111 PROVEN TECHNIQUES
AND STRATEGIES
FOR GETTING THE JOB INTERVIEW

111 PROVEN TECHNIQUES
AND STRATEGIES
FOR GETTING THE JOB INTERVIEW

BURDETTE E. BOSTWICK

JOHN WILEY & SONS
New York • Chichester • Brisbane • Toronto

Library of Congress Cataloging in Publication Data:

Bostwick, Burdette E
    111 proven techniques and strategies for getting
the job interview.

    Includes index.
    1. Employment interviewing. I. Title.

HF5549.5.I6B67   650.1'4   80–26454
ISBN 0–471–07762–3

Printed in the United States of America

10 9 8 7 6 5 4 3 2 1

To
Alexandra Bostwick Bishko
our first grandchild
born November 14, 1978

Acknowledgment

I am indebted to Wiley Editor Michael Hamilton for help in planning this book, to Publisher Walter Maytham, always hovering in the background with good advice, who offered me my first opportunity to write a book, way back in 1976; and to Wiley Board Chairman W. Bradford Wiley.

Contents

Introduction

This book is the result of new research on the subject of finding a job. It reveals in crystal clear fashion the secret of attaining hard-to-get interviews. I have excluded subjects covered in other books;* this book assumes that you are already somewhat sophisticated in the general areas of the successful job search.

I have written it because there are so many misconceptions, and so much bad advice is offered, to people needing help not hindrance. The need to get interviews is at the beginning of every job search. After the interview is secured, there is the need to know what to say. This book covers both areas with much material not heretofore known or published so far as I am aware. There is a compendium of 111 ways to get interviews that is, I think, the first effort to discover and put in one place the varied and effective ways to reach the interview objective. Most of the methods discussed are of immediate effect; some have a delayed action; others are components, which, taken together, are contributory. For example, a simple idea like using good stationery for letters and résumés won't by itself generate interviews, nor will good typing and a good physical format, but taken together they just might cause a reader to have a second look and decide to set up an interview rather than discard the candidate. Face the fact that when an attractive position is advertised, the advertiser may get a thousand résumés and inevitably only the best, perhaps 1 or 2 percent, will survive to merit the decision to interview.

In addition to identifying ways to get interviews, I have conducted my own survey to determine what causes recruiters at any level, from employment manager to president, to grant interviews to some candidates and not to others. This survey enables the job candidate to *know* the right road to his or her objectives rather than being unsure and hesitant, as in trying to find a little known town in an unfamiliar state. My experience suggests that when people know they are right they can proceed

* You might want to see *Resumé Writing: A Comprehensive How-To-Do-It Guide* and *How to Find the Job You've Always Wanted*, by B. E. Bostwick, both published by John Wiley and Son.

under a full head of steam; when they are unsure they proceed hesitantly.

The other aspect of this book is, of course, the matter of interview techniques. It tells you what to expect and explains how you should prepare yourself, including some perhaps amusing anecdotes about what not to do.

If you are looking for a new job or a new career, it would be helpful if your spouse or an interested companion read this book in order to gain an understanding of the support needed to carry out the difficult and often frustrating search.

Finally, please note that any advice that suggests a unilateral approach to the job search—throw away your resumés; quit your job before starting your search; address yourself to just a few companies; or, as one book says, "follow my interview precepts and it will make no difference what your experience or qualifications are you will get this job"—is spurious. The successful job search uses a combination of methods, selected for their appropriateness for you.

This book gives you the combination to the safe in which good jobs are kept.

I

Pathways to Interviews

A BLUEPRINT

RATIONALE FOR THE BOOK

People looking for jobs are of two kinds: those already employed but looking for a different position or new career, and those unemployed or about to be unemployed.

Based on a sampling of 2000 unsolicited résumés that, in an executive search capacity, I have been privileged to examine, employed job seekers outnumber the unemployed by almost nine to five. The preponderance of men to women submitting résumés is about 33 to 1.

There are hundreds of ways to categorize those seeking a new job. There are established executives, recent graduates, people of all ages, women entering the job market for the first time, career changers, those with high qualifications and those who are mediocre or unqualified, people with M.B.A.'s or other advanced degrees and those with little formal education, people who want to move geographically and those who are nailed to one place.

There is no single job-finding technique that suits all kinds of people. There are *tools* that all use commonly, but techniques vary from person to person. What is successful for one person may fail for another. For example, if you are employed, you are precluded from using methods that require extensive personal time, such as making broad personal contacts to create interviews, conducting an intensive telephone campaign, calling on personnel departments, or researching geographical areas and companies. If you are employed, you must rely on word-of-mouth, advertised job openings, and other kinds of communication to let employers know of your availability; or focus your attack on particular companies for which you would like to work or for whom you are specially qualified to work.

If you are unemployed, you can and must use a larger selection of methods, but you are still limited to systems that are suitable to *your* needs. *You must structure your campaign to fit yourself.* The level of your job, your net worth, family and school considerations, geographical preference, and many other conditions affect the nature of your campaign. Any advice that suggests that there is a single method for a job search, suitable for everyone, has to be bad advice.

However, there are *tools* you can use that are common to 99% of all job searches. The tools must be as sharp as possible to cut through the armor of initial negativeness that is the protection of the employer against the concerted attacks of hordes of job seekers.

The essential tools are:

1 A comprehensive effort at self-understanding, which means an organized personal search of the talents and accomplishments that express what you would be able to contribute in a job. These may be drawn from your career, education, and avocations and must be reduced to writing.

2 The translation into a résumé of the rough material you have collected. You may use methods other than a résumé to gain your objective, but it is nevertheless an essential tool to clarify your self-understanding and a basis for other writing or oral expression. You must have a résumé to respond to advertising and to utilize executive search firms or employment agencies.

3 A full understanding of the various systems of a job search, from which you create the campaign that is best suited to your needs.

4 Personal mental, psychological, and physical preparation for interviews.

5 A knowledge of the interview techniques that interviewers use, what they seek to discover, and a readiness of responses.

It is always desirable to have prepared yourself in advance for the future contingency of having to look for a job, which comes to millions of people every year with total unexpectedness.

In looking for a job there are high and low tides, either floating you or baring unexpected rocks. The tides are boom and recession, demand for particular disciplines at one time, or a period when openings for one or another skill are slack, and this varies geographically. Summer is often low tide, and so is economic uncertainty, for example, with respect to government regulations, inflation, international tension, investments, mergers, and other pervasive factors.

To look on both sides, some people find it easy to get jobs using a minimum number of techniques. Others are beset by problems. It is not unusual that getting a job or a new job requires a year of effort. This does not apply to new entrants in the job marketplace. Such companies as Corning Glass, Minnesota Mining and Manufacturing Co., and many others hire heavily at entry level but promote from within for upper-level jobs. Others say they must introduce new blood at the management level every year. On the average, over a million people are added to the work force every year, despite the percentage of unemployment. *It is helpful to remember that if unemployment is 6%, and if you are qualified, there is a 94% chance of your finding employment.* Getting the employment *you want* demands sterner measures.

A PRIORI

Successful people use "method" or "system" in everything they undertake. "Though this be madness, yet there is method in't" (*Hamlet,* act 2, scene 2). Robbing a bank or investing in the stock market or gold or real estate is a matter of learning method before acting. Setting up a curriculum needs method. Engineering is method. So is mnemonics. Writing a novel, advertising copy, or an industrial catalog demands method. Matrices and networks are systems for a logical approach to the solution of business problems. If you want to sell a painting you don't offer it to a junkman, you take it to an art dealer. If you want to sell jewelry or coins or stamps you go to an expert. If you want to create a practical but inexpensive wardrobe you use a "system" of acquisition. And so it goes for everything one does. Find the method and you are assured, inevitably, greater success.

There is little use in acquiring interview abilities if you don't get interviews. And getting interviews is a matter of method too. Here is a review or successful methods, including some of which you may not be aware.

Pete Rose, the baseball player, was the subject of a highly successful marketing campaign, which resulted in a five-year $4 million contract, the forerunner of several even more successful sales promotions by other athletes. The campaign included a film presentation that was shown to club owners and executives, TV appearances, radio interviews, extensive press coverage, and trade releases. Not many individuals could afford such a program, or would be aided by so much free coverage, but it has elements that are applicable to many people. In the trade this is called "packaging."

In looking for a job everything one does is a part of one's total package: letters, résumés, comprehensive presentations to particular companies, articles written, pictures, advertisements, speechmaking. You can give free rein to your imagination, or you can hire someone else's imagination, as Pete Rose did, to package yourself in a way that works for you. One advertising man presented himself by a résumé in the form of a menu, and was hired by a top agency. Another person took a large ad in a newspaper, complete with a picture of himself, and was successful in getting a job he wanted. Another individual advertised successfully in *Time* magazine. Many executives who have associations with public relations firms through their companies receive regular exposure through and are quoted in articles planted in newspapers and magazines, and make radio and TV appearances as well. Just as politicians may be elected by TV exposure, so executives are sometimes chosen not by interview, but by preselling through public relations devices.

Frank Borman's extensive appearances in Eastern Airlines advertising assure him favorable consideration in almost any board room, or in the voting booth—even though many advertising experts do not consider it good advertising. Bill Bradley was elected to the U.S. Senate because he was familiar to millions through television and other media as a basketball player. Even technically poor exposure is sometimes highly successful; witness the man who sells ice cream (Tom Carvel), the man who sells chickens (Frank Perdue), the lady who sells Cadillacs (Luba Potamkin), and of course the multitude of perfectly awful television commercials that still sell products.

Apparently, even sophisticated people like to be conned, so don't hesitate to use imaginative devices when job-seeking. However, tastefulness seems to be more important to the job seeker than to many corporate advertisers.

WHAT LEADING COMPANIES TELL US ABOUT GETTING INTERVIEWS

In approaching the subject of getting interviews I have personally made a survey of several hundred companies across the United States, of all sizes and types, ranging in financial size from a few million dollars to billions, to determine on what basis interviews are granted. The questionnaires used, and a compilation of the answers, are shown later in this chapter. There are actually three questionnaires: (1) entry level, (2) middle management, (3) upper management. The questionnaire was addressed by name to the top personnel officer of each corporation, titled variously Vice-President, Human Resources/Relations; Vice-President, Manpower Development; Vice-President, Personnel; Vice-President, Industrial Relations; and other titles. (Nonprofit institutions were not included.)

It is a safe assumption that over 90% of all hirings are made by personnel people. This is because over 90% of all employees of most corporations are at entry, clerical, blue collar, or middle-management levels. Labor grades were omitted from consideration in this survey. In considering total employees, however, white collar or labor, the percentage would be constant between management and all other employees. It is important to note that individuals other than personnel department officers also do some hiring. Many top and some upper middle-management executives are hired by the functional department heads: finance, marketing, production, administration, and so on, and their subordinate managers. Additionally, top and upper middle managers *influence* personnel interviewee selection and hiring. Our survey does not include these other operations but only personnel department operations and as a result certain important techniques for gaining interviews are given less than their proper importance in the survey responses. These techniques are discussed separately. Overall, the survey results confirm what I have always believed to be true, with very few surprises.

There are no gimmicks or secret methods in the successful job search. The successful job search utilizes many methods. While our survey was not intended to do so, it does destroy many of the myths promulgated by so many advisers.

The following is our questionnaire, with the accompanying instructions, as mailed to our list of companies. The pronoun "you" in the questionaire material refers to the addressee.

Explanation of Questionnaire

This questionnaire is related to *granting interviews, not to selection* of employees.

We have identified 13 commonly used approaches leading to job interviews, some initiated by a job candidate, others by an employer.

What are the approaches that influence you most commonly (or most importantly, to make the decision to grant a personal interview to a candidate, or to cause a personal interview to take place? Or to put it another way, what are the sources of your interviews, written communications, employment agencies, referrals, campus interviews, etc.?

8

QUESTIONNAIRE

Entry Level	Middle Management	Upper Management
Level 1	Level 2	Level 3
___ Advertisement ("employment wanted" ad by candidate)	___ Advertisement ("employment wanted" ad by candidate)	___ Advertisement ("employment wanted" ad by candidate)
___ Cold call on personnel department	___ Cold call on personnel department	___ Cold call on personnel department
___ College campus-initiated interviews	___ Correspondence	___ Correspondence
___ Correspondence	___ a. letter instead of résumé	___ a. letter instead of résumé
___ a. letter instead of résumé	___ b. business proposal by candidate	___ b. business proposal by candidate
___ b. business proposal by candidate	___ Direct negotiation (initiated by you)	___ Direct negotiation (initiated by you)
___ Direct negotiation (initiated by you)	___ a. utilizing résumé before interview	___ a. utilizing résumé before interview
___ a. utilizing résumé before interview	___ b. not utilizing résumé	___ b. not utilizing résumé
___ b. not utilizing résumé	___ Employment agency referral	___ Employment agency referral
___ Employment agency referral	___ Executive search	___ Excutive search
___ Referral by friend, acquaintance, or employee	___ a. initiated by you	___ a. initiated by you
	___ b. initiated by executive search firm	___ b. initiated by executive search firm
		___ Referral by friend, acquaintance, or employee

_____ Referral by other third party (someone well-known to you)
_____ Résumé
_____ a. solicited by you in "help wanted" ad
_____ b. unsolicited
_____ Telephone solicitation by candidate
_____ Other

_____ Number of interviews annually for this level
_____ Number of "hires" annually at this level
Title of hiring officer
_____

Size of your company (annual sales) _____

_____ Referral by friend, acquaintance, or employee
_____ Referral by other third party (someone well-known to you)
_____ Résumé
_____ a. solicited by you in "help wanted" ad
_____ b. unsolicited
_____ Telephone solicitation by candidate
_____ Other

_____ Number of interviews annually for this level
_____ Number of "hires" annually at this level
Title of hiring officer
_____

_____ Referral by other third party (someone well-known to you)
_____ Résumé
_____ a. solicited by you in "help wanted" ad
_____ b. unsolicited
_____ Telephone solicitation by candidate
_____ Other

_____ Number of interviews annually for this level
_____ Number of "hires" annually at this level
Title of hiring officer
_____

For example if you run an "employment available" advertisement you are initiating an interview situation, but you decide to interview specific people because of a résumé, a letter, a telephone call or otherwise. Which of the methods used by a candidate do you most heavily rely upon?

Again a candidate sends a résumé, is referred by a friend, telephones, other—what approach is most persuasive to you?

The employee job classifications involved in this survey are as follows:

LEVEL 1:   Entry level (excluding factory labor grades)
LEVEL 2:   Middle management
LEVEL 3:   Upper management

Please rank 1, 2, 3, and so on, in order of importance the determinants (activating influences, bases) which cause you to grant interviews to job candidates. You need not rank beyond five in any level, unless you wish to do so. Where a listed basis for decision is unimportant to your personnel practice, place an X in that square. Please do this separately for each of the three job levels shown. If there is an important method which you use to determine the granting of interviews, which we have omitted, please check and rank "other" and describe separately.

Please read all questions before starting answers.

Answer the additional questions relating to the size of your company, number of interviews, and number of "hires."

If you have geographical limits (location of candidate) on hiring in any of the three categories, please add this information.

Return completed questionnaire in the stamped and addressed envelope enclosed.

You need not disclose the name of your company if you prefer anonymity.

Any comments you care to make within or outside the scope of the questionnaire will be received with interest.

Your cooperation is appreciated.

Explanation of the Questionnaire Questions
As Understood by Most Respondents

Advertisement

This question refers to job candidates who run advertisements saying that they are looking for employment. Such ads are usually run in newspapers, business magazines, and trade journals under the classification "Employment Wanted." It is common, for example, for manufacturer's agents to advertise in this manner. It is possible that some questionnaire respondents could have confused this with the classification "Positions Available," but the expectedly low selection of this method as a basis for granting interviews suggests otherwise.

Cold Call on Personnel Department

This is self-explanatory.

College Campus-Initiated Interviews

This, too, needs no explanation.

Correspondence

(a) *Letter instead of résumé.* Some recruiters profess a preference for a letter. Its importance to a job candidate, however, lies outside the normal scope of personnel department practices and procedures.

(b) *A business proposal* means that a job candidate is making a specific suggestion expected to be of benefit to the addressee.

Direct Negotiation

This is initiated by the employer and may be any of the following:

1   An invited telephone call for an appointment in response to a help wanted advertisement.
2   Promotion from within.
3   Job postings by employer.
4   The employer hears of someone doing a good job for another employer, in an area where assistance is needed.
5   Meeting an attractive candidate at a convention, a business meeting, or socially who so impresses an employer that an interview is arranged.

The (a) and (b) sections are for the purpose of determining if a résumé is a document generally used in these situations or not.

Employment Agency Referral

This is self-evident.

Executive Search

(a) *Initiated by you.* This is intended to elicit a response as to the prevalence of executive search at the various job levels. The question was excluded for level 1 for obvious reasons.

(b) *Initiated by executive search firm.* Some executive search firms work on speculation and offer candidates without having an assignment to find a candidate.

Referral by a Friend, Acquaintance, or Employee

This needs no explanation.

Referral by Other Third Party

(Someone well-known to you). This is self-evident.

Résumé

Résumé (a) *solicited by employer* in help wanted advertising. This advertising is of two types, display and classified. Display advertising usually asks for a résumé or letter; classified advertising usually invites a telephone response, but sometimes asks for a résumé.

Résumé (b), *unsolicited,* refers to résumés sent to employers by job candidates who hope that a job exists and that they will be qualified for it.

Telephone Solicitation

Telephone solicitation by candidate means an *uninvited* request for an interview by a job candidate.

Other

This was an attempt to discover any bases for granting interviews not covered in the preceding questions. Where "Other" was checked in the questionnaire the answer was invariably "promotion from within," the respondents not realizing that this answer could have been included under "Direct negotiation."

LEVEL 1—ENTRY LEVEL

Employer Responses

	Method	Rank	Total Mentions	*Totals Converted to scale of 100	†Percentage
(A)	Referral by friend, acquaintance, or employee	1	615	100	18.0
(B)	Direct negotiation initiated by you using résumé before interview	2	430	70	12.5
(C)	Résumé solicited by you in help wanted advertising	3	415	67	12.1
(D)	Employment agency referral	3	415	67	12.1
(E)	College campus-initiated interviews	4	380	61	11.1
(F)	Résumé unsolicited	5	265	43	7.7
(G)	Referral by other third party (someone well known to you)	6	225	36	6.5
(H)	Correspondence—letter instead of résumé	7	185	30	5.4
(I)	Cold call on personnel department	8	140	22	4.0
(J)	Advertisement (employment wanted ad by candidate)	8	140	22	4.0
(K)	Telephone solicitation by candidate (uninvited)	9	70	11	2.0
(L)	Other	10	65	10	1.9
(M)	Direct negotiation (initiated by you) not using résumé	11	40	6	1.2
(N)	Correspondence—business proposal by candidate	12	35	5	1.0
	Totals		3420		99.5

* One hundred was assigned to the method with the highest number of mentions, and all other methods are rated against the highest.
† This is the percentage of mentions related to 100% (actually 99.5%, because the calculations were only carried to one decimal point).

13

Analysis of Level 1

At entry level by far the most common method by which one gains an interview is through referral by a friend, acquaintance, or company employee (A). It is ranked 100 and represents 18% of total mentions. If referral by a third party (G) is added with a percentage of 6.5, interview by referral increases to almost 25% (nearly one in four) as a way to gain an interview. The importance of knowing the right individual is thus highlighted.

Direct negotiation (B) assumes second place as a method of gaining interviews. Add to the 12.5% another 1.2% for "Direct negotiation not using résumé" (M), and you get a total of 13.7% to compare with the most useful method of gaining an interview (above). This category also relates to knowing someone.

"Résumé solicited in help wanted advertising" (C) is only slightly lower than "Direct negotiation" and ties with "employment agency referral" (D) as a method of gaining interviews.

"College campus interviews" (E) register as 11.1% and 61 on the scale of 100. This is a result of the broadly based survey. For many giant companies campus recruiting is a favorite method of offering interviews with a value higher than indicated.

"Unsolicited résumés" (F) result in interviews but with less than half the effectiveness of knowing someone. "Correspondence" (H), using a letter instead of a résumé, at this level is much less effective than a résumé.

"Cold calls" (I) on personnel departments are not rated high by most companies as a method of gaining interviews, but are rated number 1 by 10 companies and number 2 by 30 companies, among all methods. These companies tend to be large retailers, public utilities, insurance companies, food-related businesses, and others with a large number of clerical employees concentrated in one area.

"Uninvited telephone solicitation" (K) gets short shrift as a method of gaining interviews, although here again it ranks *first* with some companies. These companies are those seeking insurance salesmen, direct-to-consumer salespersons, commission salespeople, and franchisers; in general, companies that need hard sell to get employees rather than employers for whom applicants are plentiful.

LEVEL 2—MIDDLE MANAGEMENT

Employer Responses

	Method	Rank	Total Mentions	*Totals Converted to scale of 100	†Percentage
(A)	Résumé solicited by you in help wanted advertising	1	665	100	20.8
(B)	Employment agency referral	2	430	64	13.4
(C)	Referral by friend, acquaintance, or employee	3	415	62	12.9
(D)	Direct negotiation (initiated by you) utilizing résumé (a)	3	415	62	12.9
(E)	Executive search initiated by you	4	245	36	7.6
(F)	Résumé unsolicited	5	215	32	6.7
(G)	Referral by other third party (someone well known to you)	6	195	29	6.1
(H)	Correspondence—letter instead of résumé (a)	7	170	25	5.3
(I)	Telephone solicitation by candidate (uninvited)	8	125	18	3.9
(J)	Cold call on personnel department	9	110	16	3.4
(K)	Correspondence—business proposal by candidate (b)	11	65	9	2.0
(L)	Other	12	55	7	1.7
(M)	Advertisement (employment wanted advertisement by candidate)	13	40	6	1.2
(N)	Direct negotiation (initiated by you) not utilizing résumé (b)	14	30	4	0.9
(O)	Executive search initiated by executive search firm	15	20	3	0.6
	Totals		3195		99.4

* One hundred was assigned to the method with the highest number of mentions, and all other methods are rated against the highest.
† This is the percentage of mentions related to 100% (actually 99.6%, because the calculations were only carried to one decimal point).

15

Analysis of Level 2

At the middle management level there is a distinct change in the relative values of methods to gain interviews. The most highly rated method is by means of a résumé submitted in response to help wanted advertising (A), 20.8%.

This is closely followed by referrals if we add third party referrals (C and G) (13.4% plus 6.1%), for a total of 19.5%. Continuing to be true at this level is knowing the right individual to help you get a job, which is of great importance. Stewart Alsop, brother of the famous columnist Joseph Alsop, when asked how one can become a columnist said, "The best way to become a columnist is to have a brother who is one already."

Direct negotiation (D) and (N) together plus "Other" (L) equal 15.5%.

Unsolicited correspondence, résumés, letters, and proposals (F, H, and K), continue to hold their value at Level 2 at 14.0% and are fourth in importance. However, with respect particularly to letters and unsolicited résumés, bear in mind that much of this material is handled by functional executives other than personnel executives. Therefore the *personnel* response on these categories underestimates their importance. I think the value of these categories can be raised by at least 20%, bringing them to a real position of 16.9%, or third in practical importance to the job candidate.

Employment agency referral (B) is 13.4%. This also reflects the entrance of some employment agencies into the area of executive search.

Executive search (E) begins to have some use at middle management levels, but most employers feel that there are less expensive ways to find middle management personnel. That is what personnel departments are for, they say.

As expected at this level uninvited telephone solicitations, cold calls, candidate advertising, and speculative search (I, J, M, and O) are not, by themselves, of major value.

LEVEL 3—UPPER MANAGEMENT

Employer Responses

	Method	Rank	Total Mentions	*Weighted Totals Converted to scale of 100	†Percentage
(A)	Executive search initiated by you	1	425	100	15.3
(B)	Résumé solicited by you in help wanted advertising	2	415	97	15.0
(C)	Referral by friend, acquaintance, or employee	3	385	90	13.8
(D)	Direct negotiation (initiated by you) utilizing résumé before interview (a)	4	380	89	13.7
(E)	Employment agency referral	5	240	56	8.6
(F)	Résumé unsolicited	6	195	45	7.0
(G)	Referral by other third party (someone well known to you)	7	180	42	6.4
(H)	Correspondence—letter instead of résumé	8	140	33	5.0
(I)	Correspondence—business proposal by candidate	9	90	21	3.2
(J)	Other	10	85	20	3.0
(K)	Direct negotiation (initiated by you) not utilizing résumé (b)	11	70	16	2.5
(L)	Executive search initiated by executive search firm	12	65	15	2.3
(M)	Advertisement (employment wanted) advertisement by candidate	13	55	13	2.0
(N)	Telephone solicitation by candidate	14	50	10	1.8
	Totals		2775		99.6

* One hundred was assigned to the method with the highest number of mentions, and all other methods are rated against the highest.
† This is the percentage of mentions related to 100% (actually 99.6%, because the calculations were only carried to one decimal point).

Analysis of Level 3

If referrals (C and G) are added together (13.8% + 6.4%) they equal 20.2% and make knowing someone who can arrange an interview for you the most effective way to gain an interview.

Direct negotiation (D, K, and J) is second in importance with a total of 19.2%.

At this level, executive search (A) becomes important and moves into third place (15.3%). However, it cannot be classed as a major way to get interviews because in this process the employer is more apt to find you than for you to find him. Nevertheless, in a comprehensive job search, you must cover executive search firms with your résumé because you might be the person they are looking for and having trouble finding.

Executive search is big business, with a significant percentage of it concentrated in the hands of about six major firms. There are more than 2000 such firms across the country. They receive hundreds of thousands of résumés every year; many are consigned to the wastebasket. Others are retained for three to six months against the contingency of future search, and still others are suitable for use in a current search. People with excellent backgrounds, properly portrayed in their résumés, will get action. I suspect that unsolicited résumés play a bigger part in candidate selection than is generally admitted.

Some individuals, to my certain knowledge, have been successful in getting new positions with campaigns conducted exclusively through executive search firms. It has also happened that some small shops have selected candidates for a client without ever having met or personally screened the candidates.

Résumés sent in response to "help wanted" advertising (B) follow so closely on the leader that they give this method equal value with executive search. This is also the case with unsolicited correspondence (F, H, and J), which totals 15.0%. Since their value is underestimated by personnel executives, as a practical matter 20% should be added to give a value of 18%, close to the top. The remaining categories (L, M, and N) retain minor importance as methods of gaining interviews.

There is an unconsidered factor in top-level hiring, to be added to unadvertised available jobs. That is that some companies may be unaware of their need for a particular executive until a candidate describes his assets. In many companies several different functions may be handled by a single executive. At some time in corporate growth it becomes apparent that greater specialization might enlarge profit opportunities. Examples would be:

Merger and acquisition.

National account sales.

Special marketing classification sales (for example, an enlarging opportunity in a new or existing market).

Research and development along special lines.

A new manufacturing department.

Export sales.

Environmental problems.

Human development.

The list can be greatly expanded.

NUMBER OF "HIRES" AT THE THREE LEVELS

It is interesting to know the number of "hires" that occur out of the total number of interviews. At the entry level, the following are typical answers:

Interviews	"Hires"
5000	300
500	200
3000	300
1000	600
200	60
10	3
2000	500
3000	700
8000	1500
500	150
50,000	5000
25,000	2500
6000	400
1200	300
2000	100
15,000	5000
12,000	1200
40,000	10,000
173,410	28,813 (16% average)

Note the wide variation, from 6 to 40%.

At the middle management level, typical answers are as follows:

Interviews	"Hires"
200	45
40	10
100	20
100	20
75	20
100	23
1000	250
3000	500
4615	888 (19% average)

At this level the proportion of interviews to "hires" narrows, with an average of 16 to 25%.

Nevertheless, even if you gain an interview you still have only one chance in five of being employed.

At the upper level, the following are typical answers:

Interviews	"Hires"
6	2
12	2
30	6
15	2
100	25
200	40
363	77 (21% average)

Employment averages, as with middle management, only one "hire" for every five interviews.

TITLES OF CORPORATE HIRING OFFICERS

Entry Level

District Staff Manager.
Staff Specialist.
Personnel Manager.
District Manager, Employment.
Store Managers.
Personnel Manager (at location).
Accounting Manager.
Director of Employment.
Placement Representative.
Employment Representative.
Supervisor/Manager.

Middle Management

Staff Specialist.
Vice-President, Personnel.
District Manager.
Vice-President (functional).
Employment Representative.
Senior Employment Representative.
Manager Director.

Upper Management

Vice-President, Personnel.
President.
Vice-President, Employee Relations.
Vice-President (functional).
Placement Manager.

These data were accumulated from replies to mail campaigns by job seekers.

DEFINITIONS OF THE THREE MANAGEMENT LEVELS

In these pages I have referred to entry level, middle management, and upper management. The following broad definitions are only a general guideline and subject to refinement.

Clerical or Entry Level (Nondecision Makers)

Any job that is repetitive in character and requires a minimum of training and decision-making to administer: filing, simple arithmetic, simple bookkeeping, reception, telephone operation, office machine operation, mail department work, "gal/guy Friday" duties, billing, telex operation, and the like.

Middle Management (Decision Makers)

Lower Middle Management

Supervision of clerical workers. Assignment of duties. Monitoring productivity.

Middle Middle Management

Supervision of group of lower middle managers. Salesman, traffic manager, engineer, purchasing agent, personnel manager, and so on.

Upper Middle Management

Management of department, with some autonomous authority.

Upper Management (Tactical and Strategic Planning and Decision-Making)

Management of division or function (marketing, finance, production, legal services, personnel, etc.). Corporate officer. Director.

SUMMARY OF HIRING STATISTICS

For those who are allergic to figures, the survey results are presented in tabular form.

	I	II	III	IV
	Interviews granted as a result of written answers to advertising*	Interviews resulting from employment agency activity	Interviews as a result of direct employer/ candidate negotiation	Interviews gained through the initiative of the job candidate
Level 1	18.35%	11.5%	39.25%	30.3%
Level 2	23.6	13.4	30.2	32.0
Level 3	21.8	9.3	34.55	33.75
Rounded average	21	12	35	32

*Display, Classified, or Executive Search advertising.

Note that approximately 79% of all available jobs are filled through procedures other than advertising; however, of this 79%, 44% (79% − 35%) are internally negotiated in one way or another by employers, leaving only 56% of all unadvertised jobs available, open to the average *unsponsored* job candidate.

The survey was directed to personnel officers only, so the exceptions noted below must be considered:

1 Personnel officers are not involved in all middle management and top-level hiring; their participation may be only 75% in middle management hiring and only 25% in top management selection. They are therefore not fully cognizant of the importance of the different kinds of correspondence (letters, résumés, proposals) that motivate other functional or general managers to grant interviews.

2 The top executives of smaller companies become involved in hiring decisions to a greater extent than do those in the giant companies.

3 Sometimes opportunities exist that the employing company itself is not aware of until it discovers the capabilities expressed by a candidate—somewhat akin to a shopper's impulse buying.

From the candidate's point of view the advertising that does appear may have these deficiencies:

1 No vocational fit.
2 Inadequate compensation.

3 Unsuitable employer or product.

4 Insufficient number of suitable openings advertised.

5 Misrepresentation in the advertising.

These deficiencies serve to expand the importance of relying on other avenues and stress the importance of using one's own initiative in the job search. In consideration of these factors the preceding summary may be judgmentally revised. The figures are now rounded.

Summary Resummarized

	I	II	III	IV
	Interviews granted as a result of written answers to advertising*	Interviews resulting from employment agency activity	Interviews as a result of direct employer/ candidate negotiation	Interviews gained through the initiative of the job candidate
Level 1	16%	14%	39%*	31%
Level 2	20	13	30	37
Level 3	20	8	32	40

* Including college campus interviews initiated by employers.

THE IMPORTANCE OF WRITING

In looking for your first job or any job at clerical or lower middle-management levels, physical activity is at its most intense level: cold calls on personnel departments, telephone calls, reading the "help wanted" ads and following them up, mailing résumés, calling on friends and friends of friends. As you rise in level of responsibility and seek a new position, planning becomes more important, particularly *writing*. I believe that a successful search for an upper-level management position *demands* preparation in writing, and the use of that writing.

1 Analyze your objectives and qualifications, what you do best, what you want to do, and write it down.

2 Organize and discipline yourself by writing down your accomplishments.

3 Prepare the best written presentation of your qualifications that you can accomplish, even if you never use it. The writing will discipline your thinking. Your writing will eventually take one or more forms:
    (a) A résumé.
    (b) A covering letter.
    (c) A sales letter or broadcast letter.
    (d) A business presentation.
4 Circulate by mail and in person the fact of your availability.
5 Prepare for and know how to conduct yourself in an interview, writing down your answers to the most important questions *in advance.*

The better you express yourself in writing, where you use writing to gain interviews, the more attractive you will be to a reader. Logical presentation, clear thinking, and literate exposition used to tell another what you can accomplish (based on what you have achieved) are the methods of measurement used by a prospective employer.

If you have not done it before, don't just write a résumé or a letter blindly; learn how to do it. If you don't *learn* the rules, your writing will be poor and you will reduce your chances of gaining interviews by 50–75% or more.

How does one learn? See a qualified adviser or read a good book* on the subject. Even though some examples are provided in this book, such an inquiry will be worth a thousand times its cost.

To guide you in organizing your thinking about yourself a personal questionnaire is provided in the following pages. Unless you are very lucky, no campaign for getting a job can be conducted without extensive analytical writing about yourself.

ANALYZING YOUR JOB BACKGROUND

The key to a successful résumé is the analysis and listing of your responsibilities and achievements in an orderly manner. That is, you must know about yourself: what you were or are supposed to be doing, what you actually did or are doing, and the effect of your actions on your own work, your section, your department, your division, and your company or organization.

The analytical questionnaire presented below will help you to orga-

---

* Comprehensive treatment of writing is to be found in B. E. Bostwick, Resume Writing: A Comprehensive How-To-Do-It Guide, 1976, Finding the Job You've Always Wanted, 1977, How to Find the Job You've Always Wanted, 1979, Wiley, New York.

nize this type of information about yourself. It has been carefully prepared to make you think about yourself, to recall to your mind activities that you may have forgotten, and to help you focus on the important aspects of your vocational life. First, you must recall; then you must express your recollections. It is easier to express yourself properly after you have accomplished the first task of remembering and writing down the things you have done. This first writing can be informal—put down words, phrases, and sentence fragments, which will provide the basis for proper exposition when you start to write your résumé. It is *essential* that you do this exercise.

Analytical Questionnaire

1   Your name, address, and home and office telephone numbers.
2   Titles of jobs desired, if possible. If you cannot supply them at this time, briefly *describe* the job you want. Identify several jobs by assigning to them the Letters A, B, C, and so on, using the same code in Question 3 below.
    Turn to Question 11 and answer it before answering the questions that follow.
3   Qualifications that *you* believe you have for the jobs A, B, C, and so on, listed in Question 2. (Expanded data should be used in answer to Question 11.) *For example,* if your answer to Question 2 is "sales manager," you might answer Question 3 (you are competent to) as follows:
    (a)   Appraise pricing and distribution policies.
    (b)   Recruit and train sales staff.
    (c)   Maintain distributor liaison.
    (d)   And so on (list your most important qualifications related to your objectives).
4   Your age, marital status, number of children, home ownership, car ownership, and so on.
5   Military service.
    (a)   Dates, branch of service, rank.
    (b)   Special training, courses, responsibilities.
6   Education—dates, schools, academic degrees, and proficiency in languages.
7   Major and minor courses. List courses relevant to the jobs desired. State your class standing if possible. Describe scholarships, awards, and honors.

8 Extracurricular activities at school (sports, jobs, social activities, etc.).

9 Hobbies and your degree of proficiency in them, travel (if extensive), memberships in societies and community activities.

10 A summary of your employment history. *Work backwards,* giving the last job first. Use three columns to assemble the following information:

Dates of beginning and
leaving job (years only)   Company and address   Job titles

11 For each job listed above, starting with the *last* job, give the following data. Treat each position or important assignment with the same company, or with important clients of your employer, as though it were a separate and distinct job. Answer *each* question carefully.

(a) Job title.

(b) Dates of beginning and leaving job (by transfer to another company, or by promotion, or change within a company, etc.).

(c) Name of company and division or department within company.

(d) Description of what the company makes, sells, or does.

(e) An indication of size of company—by sales volume, number of employees, number of plants, and number of branches or stores, for example.

(f) The title of the person for whom you worked (president, foreman, sales manager, etc.).

(g) The number of persons you supervised (if any).

(h) The kinds of employees you supervised (engineers, clerks, etc.).

(i) The types of equipment you used (or that were used under your supervision) and for what purpose. This will be relevant for such jobs as production manager and computer executive, but irrelevant for others.

(j) Your responsibilities. Describe them briefly but fully; give facts, rather than abstract generalities.

(k) Your accomplishments. Describe them briefly but specifically.

• The problems you were faced with.

• What you did about them.

• What you achieved and how.

That is, what did you see that needed to be done, what did you do about it, and what happened as a result? Do not list mere claims, such as "I increased sales." Give facts: "I found that sales were only $150,000. I made a market survey and determined that the market needed a smaller sized cartridge. I introduced such a new product. I trained salesmen by making calls with them. Sales increased in six months by $50,000." Such an analysis is important. You need it in your résumé if you are to stand out from other job applicants. It will also reassure you that you are qualified for the job you want, in addition to refreshing your memory and providing valuable *rehearsal and training* for your job interviews.

Answering the Analytical Questionnaire

The two sample answers to this questionnaire appearing below illustrate what you should *not* do. Here is how one man answered Question 11:

1972–present (name of company). AREA SUPERVISOR. Began February 1972 as restaurant manager in failing unit. The unit started to show profit after four weeks. I was promoted to supervisor of two units after three months. In the following months I was given the entire Maryland area to supervise (five units). A new type of concept was developed, and I was picked to bring it into a profitable operation. At that point the larger volume (Philadelphia) units were given to me to supervise. At my request, I was moved to the New York area as supervisor in July 1973. Since that time I have opened three large-volume units for the chain, both in New York and in Pennsylvania. All of the six units now under my supervision gross $1 to $1.5 million per year.

This very successful man needed much prodding before supplying additional information vital to his case. In the final résumé below the portions with data initially not disclosed are underlined. Prod yourself for the type of detail that, as demonstrated below, can turn a poor résumé into an effective one. What did you see that needed to be done? In this case the corporation was in need of profitability. What did you do about it? In this case the man created better cost concepts. What happened as a result? In this case the units became profitable.

1972–present (name of company)
    AREA SUPERVISOR for a rapidly growing, limited menu, full service, $30 million AMEX-listed restaurant chain with 30 loca-

tions; earlier single-unit manager. Responsible for New York and Pennsylvania area supervising six $1 to $1½ million units, each with a staff of 60 to 90 people.

— Indoctrinated company with new cost concepts, which have contributed significantly to rapid growth from nine units in 1971 to 30 units currently.

— Reduced food cost from 40% to 35%.

— Opened three large-volume units; hired, trained complete staffs, installed systems.

— Accustomed to exercising controls through analysis of computer printouts daily on food, liquor, payroll. Trained managers in use of cost analyses.

Earlier managed failing unit; turned it from loss to profit in four weeks by exercise of proper controls, by establishing incentive system, and by gaining cooperation of employees. Personally contributed to success of 15 of existing 30 units and set standards for entire operation.

In our second example of how *not* to answer the analytical questionnaire the subject took a shortcut. The result again was the omission of vital information.

1 John Abrams, 367 Pasadena Ave., Pasadena, Calif. Home (123) 456–7890. Office (321) 654–0987.

2 Sales manager.

3 (a) Style of line.
   (b) In charge of all shipping.
   (c) Distribution of goods to the factory—what goes into work at the machines.
   (d) Production.

4 36—married—3 children—own home and car.

5 U.S. Naval Reserve 1956–64—2 years active—6 years reserve.

6 High school graduate—4 years—with some college.

7 Academic.

8 Worked in specialty shop—worked in bowling alley. Sports— bowling, football, baseball, horseback riding.

9 Horseback riding, photography.

10 Seventeen years in the employ of Toni Co., 1958–1975.

11 (a) Sales manager.
    (b) 1958–1975.
    (c) $45 week to $560 week.
    (d) Sales department.
    (e) Ladies' ready-to-wear.
    (f) 35 employees—$4,500,000.
    (g) President.
    (h) Supervised up to 10 employees.
    (i) Salesmen, shipping clerks, production workers.
    (j) Sewing machines, cutting machines, taping machines.
    (k) Making sure all machines were running in proper order.
         Responsible for putting them in proper order if not
         working. Selling, getting orders by phone out of town.
         Getting merchandise from the factory in time to ship
         goods. Getting piece goods in on time as per delivery
         order. Consistently, I had to be after these people to get
         the goods I needed to run the business in a proper
         manner.
    (l) In the 17 years I was with the company, I worked up
         from delivery boy to sales manager. The achievement of
         being able to book $1.0 to $1.21 million a year.

The man omitted the following important information:

1 Business increased from $2 million to $3.5 million during his tenure.
2 The business was discontinued because of the owners' retirement.
3 The company had a sales showroom in conjunction with the factory,
   where he accomplished a lot of selling to out-of-town buyers.
4 He was in charge of purchasing, inventory control, and sales forecasting and was production manager in addition to being sales
   manager.
5 He supervised seven salesmen operating nationally and reported to
   the president.
6 His association with buyers was such that he could book large orders
   by telephone.
7 He was an excellent salesman himself, in addition to successfully
   managing a sales organization.
8 He personally sold to most of the major Los Angeles and other West
   Coast department stores and was responsible for getting business
   from such national accounts as Sears, Ward, and Penney.

IDENTIFYING YOUR ACCOMPLISHMENTS

Many job applicants find it difficult to identify accomplishments they consider worthy of writing about. Doing their jobs day by day, they fail to perceive that the completion of daily tasks results in achieving certain goals, such as expedited work flow, more timely reports, improved customer service, reduction in complaints, greater productivity, and better morale.

Almost everyone has accomplishments if he will search for them. Accomplishments can be culled from avocations as well as vocations. The following list may help you identify yours. You:

- Increased profits.
- Increased sales.
- Improved work efficiency.
- Saved money.
- Reorganized.
- Reduced staff.
- Earned additional income (for employer).
- Improved competitive position of company.
- Devised new products, improved existing products.
- Expanded markets.
- Arranged financing (for company).
- Increased value of corporate securities.
- Trained.
- Solved problems.
- Contributed new ideas.
- Reduced overdue accounts.
- Reduced inventory.
- Increased turnover.
- Improved financial reporting.
- Found acquisitions.
- Reduced taxes.
- Improved management reporting.
- Reduced employee turnover.
- Used cost-saving purchasing techniques.
- Discovered better copy theme.

- Introduced better filing system.
- Increased typing speed and accuracy.
- Relieved boss of administrative details.
- Planned better meetings.
- Improved employee morale.

TAILORING YOUR PERSONAL JOB SEARCH

The techniques by which one gains interviews are exactly the same for recruiters outside the personnel department as for the personnel department recruiters, but with different emphases. My point is that under some circumstances it is more suitable that you bypass the personnel department, while in other circumstances it is desirable that you do use the personnel department.

The various techniques for creating interviews under a variety of circumstances are reviewed in Chapter 2, "111 Ways to Get Interviews."

The following comment is taken from the statement of policy of an executive recruiting firm: "Verifying credentials is perhaps the most important step in qualifying candidates. All too often candidates misrepresent their accomplishments, their past earnings, and even their educational backgrounds."

II

111 Ways to Get Interviews

MAIN ROUTES AND LITTLE-KNOWN ROADS

THE EIGHT GENERIC WAYS TO GAIN INTERVIEWS

Though there are scores of methods for gaining interviews—we define over 100—there are only eight generic ways:

1   Know someone with hiring authority or influence.
2   Use the good offices of a third party who can arrange an interview.
    (a)   An influential person.
    (b)   An employment agency.
    (c)   An executive search firm.
3   Write, asking for an interview.
    (a)   Résumé.
    (b)   Letter.
    (c)   Proposal.
    (d)   Other.
4   Telephone.
    (a)   Asking for interview.
    (b)   Following up on a letter.

5   Do something that causes you to be invited to an interview on the initiative of a recruiting executive.

6   Call at a hiring office.

7   Advertise.

8   Attend campus recruiting sessions and open houses.

All methods depend upon either speech or writing; all culminate in interfacing with another person (at the actual interview).

The methods described are of four kinds:

1   Complete actions, sufficient by themselves to lead to interviews.

2   Contributory (pieces of) actions adding up to affirmative response, but not by themselves creating interviews.

3   Suggestions relating to the environments in which you need to place yourself to gain interviews.

4   Strategies helpful in enhancing your response ratio.

In the context of your working life, everything you have done and are doing is either positive or negative with respect to getting interviews— your job history, education, cultural development, personality development, attitude, appearance, expressiveness. Similarly, everything you do from now on will be positive or negative with respect to generating interviews.

In this book we give you positive steps and methods to reduce negatives to the minimum.

Sleeves, necks, skirts, bodices, and collars cut to a pattern are useless by themselves; put together, they make a dress. The dress then fits well or badly according to the care and skill you have used in following directions.

Not all the methods mentioned are suitable for all readers. Various steps are relevant only to certain levels of jobs or to certain kinds of people. All suggestions, however, are methods that you should be aware of to stimulate your own thinking.

The discovery of methods by which to gain interviews is the result of considerable research. All the methods listed have worked for somebody. Some methods are complete in themselves; others are contributory. In other words, some methods will, of themselves, get you an interview; others will contribute 10%, or 20%, or more, toward the chances of getting an interview. Among more than 90 million people in the work force there may easily be a million variations on these themes. The listing of methods has not been done before, so far as I know. It represents not only ideas that have worked for others but also a source to stimulate your own generative processes. It is intended that most, but not all, methods will be suitable for most readers. However, some methods have special applicability to certain vocations more than others. Listed on the following pages are the most common general vocational classifications and the method numbers having such special applicability. You may find other unspecified methods of equal or greater importance to you personally.

INDEX OF MAJOR VOCATIONAL CLASSIFICATIONS
AND LEVELS OF EMPLOYMENT

Accounting	See 1, 2, 3, 4, 12, 14, 23, 70
Administration (nonprofit)	See 1, 2, 3, 4, 12, 14
Advertising (agency)	See 1, 2, 3, 4, 9, 12, 14, 45, 96, 99, 103
Architecture	See 1, 2, 3, 4, 12, 14
Banking	See 1, 2, 3, 4, 12, 14, 15, 22, 40, 77, 93
Clerical	See 4, 5, 12
Communications	See 1, 2, 3, 4, 12, 14, 15
Credit and collection	See 1, 2, 3, 4, 5
Data processing	See 1, 2, 3, 4, 12, 89
Distribution	See 1, 2, 3, 4, 12
Economics	See 1, 2, 3, 4, 12, 14, 15
Editorial	See 1, 2, 3, 4, 7, 12, 14, 15, 96
Engineering	See 1, 2, 3, 4, 6, 10, 40, 52, 88
Entry	See 1, 2, 4, 5, 10, 12, 16, 33, 84, 88
Fashion	See 1, 2, 3, 4, 10, 12, 14, 15, 52
Financial management (except accounting)	See 1, 2, 3, 12, 14, 15, 22, 40, 77, 93
Food/restaurant	See 1, 2, 3, 4, 12, 14
General management	See 1, 3, 7, 9, 14, 15, 22, 23, 30, 34, 35
Government	See 1, 2, 3, 4, 12, 32, 82, 83, 90
Hotel/motel	See 1, 2, 3, 4, 7, 12, 14
Import/export	See 1, 2, 3, 4, 8, 9, 12, 14
Law	See 1, 2, 3, 4, 12, 14, 15, 77

Manufacturing/production management	See 1, 2, 3, 4, 8, 12, 14, 15, 22, 40, 93
Management in general	See 1, 3, 4, 6, 7, 13, 14, 15, 22, 23, 24, 25, 30, 34, 35, 73, 93
Marketing management	See 1, 3, 4, 7, 8, 9, 14, 15, 22, 35, 40, 93, 96
Operations	See 1, 2, 3, 4, 12, 14
Over 65	See 1, 2, 3, 4, 12, 14, 15, 43, 49, 51, 91, 112
Personnel/industrial relations	See 1, 2, 3, 4, 12, 13, 14, 15
Public relations	See 1, 2, 3, 4, 7, 45, 96
Publishing	See 1, 2, 3, 4, 7, 13, 14, 15, 64, 96
Purchasing	See 1, 2, 3, 4, 8, 12, 13, 14, 15
Retailing	See 1, 2, 3, 4, 5, 10, 12, 13, 14, 15, 108
Sales	See 1, 2, 3, 4, 7, 13, 14, 15, 64, 96
Scientific/technical	See 1, 2, 3, 4, 12, 14, 15, 40, 42
Temporary	See 1, 2, 3, 4
Traffic	See 1, 2, 3, 4, 12, 14, 42
Warehousing	See 1, 2, 3, 4, 12, 14, 42
Word processing	See 1, 2, 3, 4, 12, 14

1

Building Your Acquaintance Directory

You will build a base of referrals by personal or written solicitation of everyone you know who could be influential in locating a job for you, introducing you to someone else who could be influential, or offering helpful advice. Make a list and use it. Leave a résumé with people who show interest. The key word is "exposure." Use this as a checklist and start a file for future follow-up.

_____	Family
_____	Friends and acquaintances
_____	Club members (athletic, fraternal, political, country, fraternity, sorority)
_____	Place of worship associations
_____	Your personal accountant and partners
_____	Your lawyer and partners
_____	Your physician
_____	Your dentist
_____	Your banker
_____	Your broker
_____	Neighbors
_____	Neighborhood stores or services
_____	Advertising agency executives
_____	Consumer magazine space salespersons
_____	Trade magazine space salespersons
_____	Trade magazine editors and publishers
_____	Trade association directors or executive secretaries
_____	Politicians
_____	College friends and acquaintances
_____	Your college placement office
_____	Community agencies or boards with which you work

_____ Members of boards of directors with whom you are acquainted
_____ Real estate dealers with whom you are acquainted
_____ Buyers and merchandise managers of wholesalers, department stores, and other large retailers
_____ Salesmen of your acquaintance

Not everyone has an index mind that will produce a list of friends and acquaintances on call. How often has it happened to you that you have asked someone, "Do you know anyone at so and so?" only to be answered in the negative. A few minutes later, however, your friend says "Wait a minute! I do know someone there. He used to eat at my old luncheon club. Sure, Bill Jones; he's a vice-president." How often have you gone to a vacation resort or traveled on a ship or airplane, knowing no one, only to discover that someone you meet is a friend of a close friend or acquaintance? Or a college roommate of a friend? Yet your friend has never mentioned him (or her), and possibly hasn't even seen him in 10 years. All of us know more people than we think we know and it takes an effort of memory to stimulate the mind into reviewing its acquaintance index.

This is the reason for the preceding. It is intended to simulate responses from the people you know (in much the same way an insurance salesman prospects) and it can be a gold mine. I know a lot of people at a local golf club casually, but well enough to talk to about the latest newspaper headline, the stock market, the condition of the golf course, or any number of subjects—including a request for information. If I phoned them, they'd know who I am, and vice versa. I was curious enough to check off the people I knew in the club roster of members and to find out their business associations. I discovered that many of them work for companies that are household names, while others are lawyers, doctors, brokers, bankers, or owners of small businesses. I was amazed at the great variety of possible sources of information I had uncovered—of which I could avail myself—and of whom I could even ask small favors, if I wanted to. Using each family member, friend, or acquaintance to explore contacts—who knows what you could end up with, probably hundreds of possible contacts, both local and out of town.

If you are a man (and free to have this kind of interest), think of it this way. You commute by train to your office every day. Each day you see the same attractive young lady on the same train. You don't know her. Your eyes may sometimes meet each other's but slide past. You wouldn't want to be rebuffed. She doesn't want to be "picked up." But one day you meet a friend on the station platform who is talking to that same young lady. He casually says, "Meet Linda Lee," and you acknowledge each other. Three simple words have completely altered a relationship. From that point on acquaintanceship can progress to any point that may be of mutual interest.

It is the same in other circumstances. Getting information or help from someone you don't know is like climbing a wall. Getting information or help from someone you know or are introduced to is like suddenly having the wall become a downhill slide. Not everyone, of course, is willing to be helpful, particularly if business is involved, because when one intercedes one assumes some responsibility, and no one wants to rashly risk the possibility of having his reputation sullied. However, you will find some people who have no hesitancy. In fact, all of us have admirers, often in the most unexpected places, among people we hardly know. I have had the experience of having greater favors extended to me by the merest acquaintances than by close friends.

A few special comments are apropos. If you work for, or formerly worked for, a company that has an advertising agency, the agency executives have contacts among their clients and others who could be useful to you. Magazine space salesmen (or saleswomen) meet hundreds of people and are often a mine of information about companies and executives. One trade magazine salesman whom I knew kept a file of employment openings in companies he did business with and acted as a kind of employment broker. He did this as a hobby, which also of course sometimes produced some new accounts.

Trade association officials receive highly confidential information from members, including personnel revelations. They often know of openings that are about to occur even before they become common knowledge in the companies. Trade magazines carry help wanted advertising, which is particularly significant to anyone in that industry. Additionally, employment wanted advertising, as opposed to help wanted advertising, is more effective in these journals than in the big newspapers. Real estate dealers often know about transfers or job changes of business executives. Transfers "out" mean openings "in." Buyers (hardware wholesalers, department stores, and so on) know who the good salesmen are, who the poor ones are, which companies are well represented and which are not. They can be helpful in two ways: recommending good salesmen to companies that are looking for them and identifying companies with poor representation, where you might make application. Salesmen collect lots of information. If your career is in sales, get to know others in this fraternity—it is a mutual aid society, and not only at the sales level. Bankers, investment counselors, accountants, and board members all have confidential lines into the innermost plans of corporations. Depending on what you have to offer, it could be invaluable for you to meet and talk with them.

The truth is that you never know who might be able to help you until you ask, and assistance can come from the most unexpected sources. The job marketplace is like a fraternity that in a sense excludes those it does not know, but accepts all who know the password, "Meet Linda Lee." This does not mean that knowing the right person is the only way to get a job; it does mean that it is one of the best ways.

Caveat

Even though the easiest way to get a job is to know someone with the influence to provide it, this method is not necessarily best for the candidate. Relatives often get jobs for which they are unqualified. Businesses have been ruined by nepotism. A relative might be well advised to make it on his or her own before returning to a family business. There are always exceptions, of course; sometimes the younger generation exceeds its forbears in good management.

Getting a job through the good offices of another sets up obligations that may become embarrassing at some point; or may place you in the wrong job in terms of your career; or in the wrong company or geographic location; or the job may be more restrictive than one you would prefer or accept under free-choice conditions. For these reasons, use friends and acquaintances to gain interviews but remember that, if possible, you are seeking to be able to make choices, not just get a job.

Help Wanted Advertising

In looking for a job if you don't know someone who can give you a job, the first place to search is the help wanted advertising in the major metropolitan newspapers. These openings exist, and an interview is usually assured if you are qualified.

The New York Times and *The Wall Street Journal* have national circulation and are considered the most important media for advertising job openings. The *Journal* publishes a weekly compendium of the advertisements that have appeared in all of its editions, the *National Business Employment Weekly*. There are, of course, specialized newspapers, such as *Variety* and *Back Stage* for the performing arts.

The New York Times has three sections on Sunday in which job openings are advertised:

1 Classified help wanted advertising—a section by itself. These advertisements are generally for lower level jobs.
2 Display help wanted advertising—found in the Business and Finance section. These advertisements are generally for management positions.
3 "Careers in Education," located in *The Week in Review* section in Sunday editions.

The classified advertising section contains ads placed by employers seeking employees and the advertising of employment agencies. Most classified advertisers invite a telephone response.

Display section advertisers and those who advertise offering careers in education require a résumé before an interview (87%).

2

Help Wanted Classified Advertising

The classified advertising section is so bulky that few people ever analyze it. One can refer only to his own job category and fail to find similar positions offered, though they may be listed elsewhere. A typical edition of *The New York Times* on Sunday contains approximately 3000 classified help wanted advertisements placed by employers and perhaps an equal number of advertised job openings by employment agencies. Many of the company advertisers are smaller than the multimillion-dollar employers I surveyed. The agency advertisements try to fill the employment needs of both small and large corporations for their clerical and lower and middle management openings. Many big employers work closely with employment agencies for original screening of job candidates.

The following is taken from an article by Donald H. Sweet, Manager of Employment at the Celanese Corporation, in *EMA Reference Guide,* Annual Edition, 1979, published by the Employment Management Association. It is called How to Select and Effectively Use an Employment Agency:

> Selecting and effectively utilizing an employment agency is predicated basically on understanding that employment agencies earn their fees by finding jobs for individuals. They get paid when the job applicant reports to work (as opposed to the Executive Search firm which finds individuals for positions and is compensated on a guaranteed basis for time expended). Employment agencies' fees are usually controlled by state law. For maximum utilization, agencies should be permitted to operate as an extension of your office. In order to function in such a role, a relationship must be built to the point where an agency can simply call and tell you about applicants for a particular job and you, in turn, have the confidence to invite them for interviews. Thus, companies must have faith in the agency's ability to know the type of person who fits their particular environment. That in itself presupposes a lot of things, not the

least of which is that the agency is willing to devote the time to learning about the organization. To reach this ultimate relationship you must select the right agency. Thus, your effectiveness will only be as good as your selectiveness.

Choosing the right employment agency involves a number of things, not the least of which is how to use your other applicant sources such as advertising, write-ins, employee referrals, etc. Obviously, all sources available to you should be employed and it is this author's thinking that utilizing a combination of sources allows for a better relationship with a smaller and more elite group of employment agencies and a resulting economical and efficient rating for the overall employment program. This also provides a bigger carrot to the agency being considered, i.e., more exclusiveness of job listings.

The job openings advertised in the other two sections of *The New York Times* mentioned below, also run into the hundreds. Despite the multiplicity of help wanted offerings, many job seekers cannot find a match-up between what is available and their own skills. Other problems of location, people, compensation, type of company, and opportunity may not meet the requirements of the candidate. Also, jobs available may be misrepresented, and letters to employers may not be answered. For many job seekers, therefore, the help wanted advertising pages will not be suitable at all, or only partially so. The search of the help wanted pages must be supplemented by other, and frequently more effective, methods of gaining interviews. Keep in mind, too, that it is a frequently expressed theorem that 80% of the jobs available are never advertised (although my own survey does not support so high a figure). If this is so, it is due at least partly (as disclosed in my survey) to the fact that referrals by employees, friends, and others, and other methods of recruiting play an important role in candidate selection.

Nevertheless, at certain job levels employment agencies are important and a regular perusal of classified and display sections and/or the education section is mandatory for a serious job search.

Clerical jobs make up the greater part, but by no means all, of the openings advertised in the classified sections.

The jobs advertised in the display advertising section are upper level with few exceptions.

For your information, I have reviewed a typical classified section of *The New York Times* so that you may determine if it is suitable for your needs or not. The review is confined to the advertising placed by companies themselves. Employment agency advertising is similar, but broader in its offerings. Salaries in general range from $9,000 to $50,000 (as of 1980).

The ten most wanted categories are:*

1	Clerical, including part time	643
2	Engineers—all disciplines	344
3	Salesman/woman	more than 300
4	Secretaries—all types	299
5	Bookkeeper	234
6	Data processing	158
7	Gal/guy Friday	114
8	Dental assistant	105
9	Insurance	96
10	College graduates	95

The full listing appears on succeeding pages.

The following list is a sample of advertised job offerings in a typical issue of *The Sunday New York Times'* classified section.

Artist	35
Assembler	2
Bookkeeper	234
Assistant office manager	1
Assistant buyer	1
Attorney	23
Auditor	19
Auto mechanic/auto sales	20
Baker	3
Miscellaneous bank positions	33
Translator	14
Biller/typist	19
Bindery	3
Biochemist	5
Camera technician/operator	4
Carpenter	3
Cashier	8

* These account for approximately 2400 of the 3000 listings.

Finance	35
Food service	21
Foreman	21
Freight forwarding	2
French/English secretary	8
Fund raiser	9
Gal/guy Friday	114
German/English secretary	3
Graphics	3
Guards	4
Hairdressers	19
Hotel	17
IBM operators	6
Import	10
Industrial engineer	25
Insurance	96
Interior design	5
Inventory	8
Jeweler	28
Key punch operator	11
Laboratory technician	7
Law secretary	83
Librarian	16
Machine shop	15
Mail room	18
Maintenance	30
Consulting	2
Management trainee	31
Manager	36
Manicurist	5
Manufacturing manager	3
Marketing research	13
Marketing manager	15
Materials control	3
Mechanic	15
Mechanical engineer	11

Medical secretary	47
Messenger	9
Metallurgy	6
Methods engineer	2
Model	10
Nurse	43
Occupational therapist	5
Office manager	30
Offset pressman	17
Operations	1
Optician/optometrist	13
Order processing	8
Packaging	5
Paralegal	9
Part-time typist/clerk/miscellaneous	83
Payroll	18
Pension administration	3
Personnel	92
Pharmaceutical	7
Pharmacist	19
Photo	28
Photostat	3
Physical therapist	6
Placement counselor	39
Plant manager	19
Plumbing	6
Pressman	10
Printing	27
Production manager	47
Programming	121
Proofreader	14
Public relations	30
Publishing	28
Purchasing	15
Quality control	12
Real estate	17

Receptionist	16
Restaurant	29
Retail	37
Salesperson	4
Secretary	293
Security	16
Sheet metal	5
Shipping	14
Social work	20
Spanish/English secretary	8
Superintendent	20
Switchboard	13
Systems analyst	29
Teacher	28
Technical writer	13
Teletype	10
TV technician	10
Textiles	11
Tool and die	12
Traffic	5
Trainee	10
Travel agent	28
Typesetter	23
Typist	50
Vydec	10
Waiter	6
Wall Street	70
Warehouse	14
Word processing	20
Writer	7
Sales positions, separately listed	more than 300

Advertisements placed in the classified section by employment agencies are somewhat broader in classification than those placed directly by companies, and include some salaries higher than $50,000. The job classifications listed have many subclassifications relating to job levels and specific experience required.

3

Help Wanted Display Advertising

This form of advertising is ranked by personnel executives as the most important basis for selecting interviewees at middle management levels. It is ranked third in importance for upper-level management recruiting.

Much help wanted advertising is misleading and overblown. Some is not legitimate. The responses generated can be in the hundreds or thousands. Many applicants are never answered because so many other résumés are better or show more specific qualifications, or simply because the sheer magnitude of response sets up arbitrary requirements to screen out résumés for any number of reasons. Nevertheless, answering these ads is an essential method of gaining interviews.

You may answer these ads as long as four or five weeks after they have appeared. Sometimes delay in answering can be an advantage because you have avoided the period of greatest influx. Employment decisions sometimes take months to be made.

STUDY HELP WANTED ADVERTISING

Study the way help wanted advertising relating to your occupation is phrased. In writing about yourself adopt some of the wording for your own self-description.

Here are some typical advertisements:

You're skilled, bright, articulate, strong on detail, committed to achievement. You will be well matched to our search for a well-organized administrative assistant/secretary, with strong skills (s.h. 110+) for our C.E.O.

If you have these attributes and the ability to handle a great deal of independent responsibility, then this diversified, stimulating opportunity and its pace should be compelling.

Our offices are beautiful. Yours is private and looks out over a pond.

Pretty flowery, some of it. In your reply attune yourself to the ad's tone. Here's another:

Ideal candidate will have a bachelor's degree in Business Administration or Computer Science, and at least 5 years successful programming commercial data base applications experience in an IRM 370 MVS environment. Skill in use of COBOL and general report writer packages also required. Background or exposure to IMS a definite plus.

Your reply should be just as explicit.

COVERING LETTERS

Any résumé mailed in response to an advertisement must be accompanied by a covering letter. If you are answering a large number of advertisements an individually composed letter is a chore. However, if an ad seems particularly appropriate for you, or if the qualifications needed are not exactly expressed in your résumé, a covering letter directed specifically to the advertisement will give you a better chance for an interview than those who make only a general reply.

See the examples of covering letters below.

EXAMPLES OF LETTERS TO ACCOMPANY RÉSUMÉ

My job is in an unpromising department, which is the reason I am seeking new employment.

I have, however, been promoted four times in the last three years. I am now supervisor of the order department of a $10 million company (order editing, order rewriting, order tracing, credit checking, back ordering, order record-keeping), with a staff of seven clerical assistants.

During my tenure I have reduced errors in order filling by 25%, expedited deliveries from 48–72 hours to 24 hours, saved $37,000 in shipping costs, and reduced my staff by two (who were reassigned within the company). During this period I also gained a B.B.A. degree by attending evening classes.

I believe I have more to offer at age 27 than my current position offers. My résumé is enclosed. If my qualifications suggest that I could fill a need in your company, I'd welcome an interview.

Your reply will be appreciated.

Sincerely,

EXAMPLES OF COVERING LETTERS

You can use a covering letter, accompanying a résumé, to express special or personal factors relating to a particular job, company, or industry; area of interest; geographical location; or any other special condition. The use of the letter means you don't have to make changes in your more generalized résumé.

You might write:

"I am applying to your company for a position because everything I have learned about it by reading your annual reports and advertising and familiarizing myself with your products, corresponds with my personal interests and objectives."

"I am applying to you for a position because I have had successful experience in the industry, which would be of value to your company."

"I am applying to you for a position because you may have an opening in the area in which I am particularly qualified (marketing, sales, finance, engineering, personnel, other)."

"I am applying to you for a position because I am very much interested in relocating in (name of city). My reasons for this are (friends, relatives, climate, other). My qualifications are not readily found in that area (etc.)."

HOW TO ANSWER HELP WANTED
DISPLAY ADVERTISING

You will find the following ways to answer ads effective.

If you are employed and your job search is confidential you must be careful about answering "blind" ads (no company name given). The ad may have been placed by your own company. You may be able to discover the identity of a "blind" advertiser by calling the newspaper carrying the ad. You can also answer incognito, enclosing a statement of your qualifications and an explanation of the confidentiality necessary, and providing a box number for the answer.

An article in *The Wall Street Journal* (September 12, 1978) reporting on the findings of an executive search firm stated that some enlightened employers are telling employees that it is not necessary to "sneak around" in looking for a new job. They are presumably interested either in persuading employees to remain or helping them to find a new position if there is mutual dissatisfaction. (I am skeptical of the validity of this.)

If you can find out exactly what the advertiser is looking for, you can write a better letter in answer to an ad. Most job seekers do not bother to call the advertiser (if the name is disclosed), and often a telephone call to the person named or to the personnel manager will elicit valuable information. If you do make the call, be sure you avoid detailed disclosure about yourself until you find out as much about the job requirements as possible; specifics should be left for the personal interview.

The general rule in answering ads is that the more detailed you can be with respect to your qualifications for the exact job involved, the better will be your chances.

Frequently the ad itself discloses information after careful analysis that is not apparent from a first reading.

Consider the following advertisement for a senior systems programmer:

> Major job functions will require you to support communications software in a TCS/VS/CICS environment, and analyze and resolve technical problems. Your background should exhibit a detailed and complete comprehension of VS operating systems, TCAM knowledge, 3–5 years systems programming experience in an OS/VS shop, specific knowledge of CICS internals and SMP, good verbal skills, and a willingness to perform goal maintenance skills. Forward your résumé and salary history in confidence to (name of company and individual follow—a brokerage company).

This ad tells you:

1 You must have substantial experience in programming and systems packages.
2 Your experience should have been with IBM software.
3 The symbols used are all within the communications area, not in applications programming.
4 The advertiser is a brokerage company.
5 You must be able to express yourself with respect to EDP in nontechnical language understandable to general executives, and be able to write and speak clearly in providing instruction manuals and training sessions.
6 You must be constantly aware of the rapid changes in computer technology, hardware and software, and show evidence of your continuing education.
7 The age range sought is 30–35.
8 Previous experience in brokerage accounting systems will be a plus.

In answering any ad it is worthwhile to list the elements appearing in the ad, to find out (if possible) anything you are unsure of, and to incorporate in your answer everything that is relevant. To answer the above advertisement, for example, you could use a résumé like the following one, which emphasizes your familiarity with IBM equipment and the continuing professional updating of your skills. If your age is favorable, mention it—if not, omit it. In your covering letter you can refer to the fact that your verbal communications skills are high and that you have been successful in making improvements in systems more expeditiously because you have been able to clarify technical problems to executives who do not possess a computer background. In expressing highly technical qualifications a résumé is a more suitable document than a letter. In the next illustration, a letter provides an opportunity to detail background with a different emphasis than would normally be present in a résumé prepared for general use.

43 Ocean Gap   (123) 456-7890
Hermosa Beach, CA

RÉSUMÉ

JETHRO BALBOA

EDP SYSTEMS DESIGNER and ANALYST

SUMMARY

***   Qualified to design online systems, implement and
operate at optimum capacity. Record of providing
cost savings in time, manpower, and equipment and
utilizing advanced technology to accomplish objectives
within expedited time frames.

EXPERIENCE

1975–Present   Pacific Continental Telephone Co., Los Angeles, CA
ONLINE SYSTEMS DESIGN AND PERFORMANCE ANALYST for one of the
nation's largest computer installations.

Responsible for
A.   justifying and devising plan for the following:
   1.   conversion of Disbursement Accounting Department's TCAM
        (Telecommunication Access Method) data collection system to
        CICS (Customer Information Control System) and centralization
        of online programming
   2.   CICS online inquiring to IMS data bases via DL/I interface
   3.   eventual migration to mixed CICS-IMS/DC-VTAM environment and
   4.   selection of an online text editor to replace TSO for source
        program development and maintenance by application
        programmers

B. (earlier) headed task force of three analysts to improve Disbursement
    Accounting online CICS Data Entry System.
    —converted from CICS Release 1.2 to Release 1.3 and fine-tuned CICS
    —redesigned and reprogrammed the major Data Entry Application
      Module
    —established Data Entry Problem Determination procedure
    —fine-tuned CICS system to a half-second response time and cut
      CICS CPU resource requirements by 50%
    —installed PAII for work load and performance tracking and
      capacity planning
    —converted CICS 2260 terminal support to 3270 Native-Mode support

    Accomplished B. above in 6 weeks versus estimated time frame (by
    IBM) of 16 weeks.
C. initial assignment to:
    1. redesign department's Mechanized Work reporting TCAM Data
        Collection System
    2. act as team leader of four Assembly language and COBOL
        programmers during design and implementation of system

Accomplishments overall
—initiated formation of committee to determine requirements of
  Disbursement Accounting Department for next five years
—designed data collecting system that facilitated maintenance and
  provided additional flexibility
—expanded capacity of system; increased productivity by 100%,
  eliminating the need for additional hardware

1972–1975   Great Western Insurance Co., Los Angeles, CA
Senior Programmer for major insurance company.
Responsible for
—creating a work load Statistics Report program for the Online Data Entry
  System batch program to convert data entry records to card image
  record for batch processing
—INTERCOMM systems programming
—conversion of Data Entry Application Modules from 2260 to 3270
  native mode, a table-driven, basic editor for online application

1970–1972   Equimetro Life Insurance Co., Los Angeles, CA
Programmer assigned to COBOL and BAL program maintenance group
after employment as trainee.

EDUCATION AND PROFESSIONAL TRAINING
B.S., Mathematics, California Western University, San Diego, CA, 1970
Stanford University graduate training: 30 hours of Computer Applications
Information Systems (Computer Management)
IBM training includes: Performance Evaluation and Capacity Planning;
                         all CICS courses; all IMS/DC courses;
                         TCAM application and systems courses;
                         TSO training; BAL and COBOL programs;
                         3600 Finance System training, INTERCOM
                         (TP Monitor) training;
over a period of eight years.
Worked at various jobs throughout college years.
Hobbies: Basketball, track, football, chess, skiing
Personal Data: Age 30, separated, excellent health

REFERENCES AND FURTHER DATA ON REQUEST

Consider this advertisement for a specialty apparel buyer:

M. M. Deen, nationally known retail and catalog merchandiser, is expanding its buying group. Live and work in a small town near the Maine coast, mountains, and forests. Experience with traditional specialty outdoor apparel for men and women to include textiles in general, casual sportswear, and active outdoor apparel and accessories.

An exciting position you can only find in a small and professional organization. Responsibility for product development (test products on trips and expeditions), vendor selection, merchandising, buying and staff development. Position requires strong analytical skills; minimum of 3–5 years experience with major retail/catalog merchant; knowledge of fabric construction.

Attractive salary and benefits.

Write to (name of company and recruiter).

This advertisement discloses the following information:

1 Name of company and name of person to whom to write.
2 Position: apparel buyer—men and women.
3 Outdoor sporting specialties—apparel.
4 Knowledge of textiles is required.
5 It is a small but national organization.
6 Product testing ability is needed.

7 Personal outdoor interests are important.

8 3–5 years buying experience = 25–30 years of age (possibly older).

9 Retail/catalog experience (major company).

10 Basic textile buying experience desirable.

11 Degree probably expected.

12 Willingness to live in small town.

13 Analytical skills required.

From other sources you can discover that the company has a sales volume of about $30 million, is located about 15 miles north of Portland on Route 1, has 380 employees, three officers, and in addition to buying also manufactures footwear, and sporting and athletic goods. Sales per employee amount to $79,000, a high ratio, suggesting that the executives probably apply themselves to a variety of responsibilities.

It deserves an answer something like the following:

Reason for letter	This is in response to your advertisement in *The Wall Street Journal* (date).
Expression of analytical skills	In a ten-year career with Abercrombie, Sears, Penney & Co., famous national retail and catalog merchandiser, where I am presently employed, I tripled women's sportswear sales over a period of seven years, increased markup 11% and gross margin 7.5% on a total departmental volume of $75 million. During this period we have achieved a national reputation for sports and casual wear.
Describes exposure to outdoor specialty attire	I have carried out extensive research on sports apparel, fabrics, linings, weight, closures, durability, warmth, and other aspects of correct clothing for scores of activities ranging from casual use to use under the most rigorous conditions of climbing, hunting, fishing, exploring, and the like. I have also been involved in outfitting complete expeditions to the North Pole, Africa, the Himalayas, and other exotic areas.
Describes technical fabric knowledge	I have taken intensive courses at the New York School of Textile Design and am thoroughly knowledgeable about fabric wear, count, texture, sources, and the methods of achieving desired qualities according to end use.

Tells of apparel testing experience and outdoor life style	In connection with my work and for pleasure I have traveled extensively in wilderness and white-water areas and overseas to Kashmir, the lower reaches of Mt. Everest, and Kilimanjaro.
Emphasizes broad retail administrative experience	My background includes buying for both stores and catalog, merchandise presentation, distribution, automatic shipping systems, profit projections, budget administration, promotion planning, and market testing.
Gives reason for interest	I am interested in moving from a giant corporation to a less structured atmosphere where opportunity for greater career and personal development are both present.
	My résumé is enclosed.
Asks for interview	If there is a meeting of my qualifications and your need I would welcome a chance to explore it personally with you.
Asks for reply	I look forward to your reply.

Sincerely,
Ann Holmes

4

Employment Agencies

Employment agencies solicit information about job openings from employers and act as agents between employer and employee. The agency charges a fee for successfully filling a job opening—one week's or one month's salary, or more. In some cases the agency fee will come out of your pocket. Or your employer may pay the fee, depending on company policies. In most states employment agencies operate under state licenses.

Since they depend on a large turnover, employment agencies handle many lower level positions. Study the advertisements in your local newspaper to find out what kinds of positions are available and at what salary levels. Do not register with more than three or four appropriate agencies. You become undesirable from both an agency and an employer point of view if you let yourself be "multiple listed," for many agencies have the same job listings. An employment agency will want your résumé. Your discussion with an interviewer should be limited to about 30 minutes. Second and third interviews will probably be a waste of time, unless the agency requests a return visit. If you are looking for a position paying above $40,000 a year, you should generally avoid employment agencies.

However, the line of demarcation between the employment agency and the executive search firm is less clear now than it formerly was. Some employment agencies conduct search work on speculation, just as many executive search firms do; that is, if they find a person they think is highly marketable, they circulate the fact of his or her availability by telephone or letter to their correspondent companies.

Conversely, some companies seeking upper-management candidates will now go to employment agencies for assistance, thus saving money (perhaps a cost of only 10% vs. 25–33% of annual salary). The employment agency has not conducted a search; it has caught a fish by accident from the local pier. The reward is therefore less than for the search firm that conducts an intensive search (akin to salmon fishing in Scotland, complete with transportation, food, lodging, guides, and atmosphere).

The federal government as well as every state and most large city governments have publicly operated employment services. If you are interested in government service, visit these agencies. For example: The Manhattan Telephone Directory lists telephone numbers for job information, (212) 566–8700, and job applications, (212) 566–8720. Under "New York–City of" are complete listings of agencies and departments, often including headings such as employment section, bureau of personnel, personnel. "New York–State of" lists the following:

- Jobs—Household (212) 247–5010.
- Industrial construction and transportation (212) 265–2700.
- Office personnel (212) 869–8000.
- Professional placement (212) 532–1221.
- Labor Department (see extensive listings under this heading).

In the Manhattan Directory under "United States Government" there are extensive departmental listings. The Federal Job Information Center telephone number is (212) 264–9422.

5

Personnel Departments

The personnel departments of department stores, factories, insurance companies, banks, and other companies are accustomed to having job seekers telephone for appointments or walk in off the street for an interview. In an earlier time Help Wanted signs on doors were a principal way of attracting new employees; they still are in small businesses.

It remains true that at entry levels, for retail sales positions, for labor and blue-collar hiring, one may make cold calls on personnel departments with a good chance for an interview. If an interview is not immediately arranged, an appointment may be set up. For the most part, except for blue-collar hiring, it will be necessary that you have a résumé to show.

In cities where there are large pockets of unemployment, cold calls are discouraged because it would be physically impossible for a given employer to handle the number of people who might descend on him. Summer and Christmas are good seasons in which to gain temporary employment, which sometimes leads to permanent jobs.

Classified help wanted advertising is, of course, your invitation to telephone for an appointment.

If you call on a personnel department without an appointment, you will at least find out what you have to do to gain an appointment. To identify the relative acceptance value by corporations to cold calls, see the survey in Chapter 1.

6

Chambers of Commerce

Every state and major city has a Chamber of Commerce. It is a public relations function, active in promoting the business, tourist attractions, and other special characteristics of its area. It studies demographics, trends, and geographic and natural resource advantages, tries to attract business, and sometimes offers tax advantages and other incentives. The Chamber is therefore aware of much that goes on in a way in which the average area citizen isn't. The Chamber can be a great source of information for job seekers and should be among the first ports of call when visiting a new city or looking for leads in one's hometown.

Find out about corporate moves, expansions, new businesses, real estate developments, urban renewal projects, major employers, area growth rate, economic changes, ethnic balance, retail store environment. These inquiries will enable you to know more about the city than most of the residents do. It is probable that these lines of inquiry will turn up job information and lead to advantageous contacts.

7

Conduct a Campaign Aimed at a Single Company

Send a message every day for four or five days to the individual with whom you would like to have a meeting.

Accompany the message with something concrete that illustrates or symbolizes the idea you have.

Attach a brand new penny or quarter to your letter (it gets attention and is seldom resented).

Send a first-day-of-issue stamp and envelope and refer to it briefly in your message.

Send a boutonniere to a man each day for several days, a single rose to a woman.

Tape measures and yardsticks are inexpensive and can be used to symbolize many things; use them to make a point, accompanying a message.

An inexpensive pair of children's scissors might be attached to a letter to illustrate a cost-cutting idea that you have developed.

A small pencil attached to a letter is commonly used in circulation campaigns by publishers to give the addressee the idea of signing on the dotted line.

A mobile could accompany a letter to symbolize any kind of creativity.

I have been told of one job candidate who sent a pizza every day for five days to a particular executive with whom he was trying to gain an appointment. The daily pie was used to dramatize the quality of the paper wrapping. He got the meeting he sought and a successful interview.

There is the story of an individual who sent a copper plate engraving of his résumé to a copper mining company with which he was most interested in gaining employment. He had it mounted on a teakwood block and mailed it special delivery to a designated executive. He was accorded an interview and hired. The method cost $600 but was well worth it; in fact, the investment was a pittance compared with the personal future he secured.

Do not look upon your job search as a place to economize. If you can afford it, do anything productive to gain your objective.

The reproduction of a gold coin by color photocopying would draw attention to your letter or résumé, but tie it in with your message.

A book, a sculpture, a package of English or Turkish cigarettes, any object relevant to you or your idea can be used to gain favorable attention for a letter.

Start thinking along these lines and ideas will flow.

8

Industry Trade Shows

Trade shows provide not only an opportunity to exchange goods and services (buyer/seller), but also a chance to meet exhibitor headquarters' personnel and exchange ideas or uncover employment potentials.

Who attends trade shows? The salesmen and often the top executives of exhibitors, including trade magazine salesmen and editors; the buyers and top executives of the companies who visit to see what is new, and to buy; nonexhibitors who want to determine if they should participate; competitors who want to see what is new in their industries; and believe it or not, recruiters seeking meetings with potential employees.

Many executives remain apart from actual selling and attend trade shows merely to absorb information. They have time to talk and are receptive to ideas—from any source. Here are some suggestions if you attend a trade show to unearth possible job opportunities:

1 Identify your particular area of interest and concentrate on the companies in that industry.
2 Plan ahead of time what you might be able to say that would be of interest: past conversations with a mutual customer; a product complaint you have overheard; a major customer not handling the line; results of a personal survey; an idea you have had; a compliment for their display or for one of their representatives; criticism or compliment for their advertising; mutual industry problems; a recent story in a trade or business magazine or newspaper; a personnel change; an acquisition; a tip about an interested prospect not now a customer; a mutual acquaintance with a well-known executive—the possibilities are endless.
3 Introduce yourself to an executive in attendance and pursue one of these or other avenues.
4 Introduce yourself to trade magazine representatives; bring the conversation around to your interest; ask for suggestions.

5 If you have something important to say, and know the executive slightly, invite him to lunch. Many people are responsive to luncheon invitations.

Remember that meeting and talking with people lays a foundation; there need not be an immediate structure you can erect on it.

9

Conventions

Business conventions are social/work events offering plenty of opportunity to meet people under relaxed conditions conducive to informal get-togethers.

It is important to remember what has frequently been said: companies are constantly on the lookout for employees who can add another dimension to an existing staff. It may be replacement, special expertise, popularity, presence, a recognized ability (even a golfing talent).

Approach a convention environment with ideas on subjects of interest to delegates generally and specifically: new government regulations, packaging problems, pricing structure, freight, payment terms, wholesaler education, retailer or distribution problems. Make yourself an expert in some important area. When you meet people, talk to them on subjects you know must be of interest to them. Bend conversations from social to business subjects without being aggressive or pushy. Seek openings that will permit you to express your main interest: getting a job or getting a new job.

If you are not employed, the convention director can usually arrange a guest admission for you.

10

Cities Where Job Opportunities May Be Better

While New York and other older cities suffer a decline in employment and a loss of employers, Sun Belt states like Texas, Oklahoma, Georgia, and others have been enjoying boom times. Some states, like California, offer opportunities not available elsewhere just because California is different, or because of the concentration of certain industries such as advanced electronics (or sailplaning). The pendulum swings and New York will eventually return to its position (if it ever lost it) as the greatest center for employment in the world.

Depending upon your field, you might find it easier to get the job you want in another area. While construction work is declining in one area, it is growing in another. The same is true of teaching, nonprofit work, new plant openings, electronics, boatbuilding, aircraft construction, and motion pictures.

11

Paying Your Own Travel Expenses to an Interview

One does not always find satisfactory employment opportunities in one's immediate neighborhood. Often more attractive opportunities occur far from one's hometown.

If you are at an upper-management level, distance from your target is no problem; the potential employer is happy to pay your travel expenses to an appointment.

If your job level is lower, however, employers will prefer to hire locally. Be ready to assume your own travel expenses if the employment opportunity is attractive and you detect real interest in you.

If you are planning to relocate to another geographical area, you should write in advance to suitable employers and set up a time when you will be available for an interview.

You can gain interviews if you are willing to pay your own expenses.

One individual living in Canada was eager to relocate somewhere in Australasia, preferably Australia or New Zealand. He had resigned from his job and decided to take his family to the region on vacation. By writing well in advance and naming specific dates in his itinerary when he would be available, he was able to set up a series of interviews in major Australian and New Zealand cities and in American Samoa.

12

Mailing Résumé with Covering Letter

At both entry and middle management levels, the mailing of an unso-licited résumé is a favorite basis upon which companies decide to grant interviews.

A mass mailing of résumés (with accompanying letter) is a most ef-fective way of locating unadvertised openings and gaining an invitation to an interview. It seems well established that over 50% of all the jobs available are not advertised. Our survey tells us why: Employers find em-ployees through referrals, employer-initiated interviews, from cold calls by candidates, and by other methods, so that frequently they do not need to advertise. Jobs do not open up everywhere at the same time; but they open up somewhere all the time. You are chancing that your résumé will arrive at the right time in perhaps 5% to 10% of the com-panies you address. If you send out 200 résumés you might get 10 or more invitations to come for an interview.

At entry level you should send your résumé to the employment direc-tor, by name.

At the middle management level you have a choice. You can mail your résumé to the personnel department (director, by name) or to a functional vice-president or manager (functional, e.g., marketing, finance, production, law, international, etc.). Your résumé may be referred to personnel or may prove interesting to another addressee, with a recom-mendation to interview. Such a recommendation will be almost surely acted upon affirmatively. You most probably will be screened by a per-sonnel representative before reaching a functional executive.

If you are at an upper middle management level, you may want to substitute a broadcast letter for a résumé. In any event do not under-estimate the value of mailing an unsolicited résumé.

RÉSUMÉ FORM

Select the résumé form most suitable for you. A résumé for an ad-ministrative position in a nonprofit institution is completely different from a résumé for a job in private industry. A résumé for an entry-level position is completely different from one for an individual with a lot of job experience. A career-change résumé is different from other résumés. A professional résumé is different from a commercial résumé. A generalist's résumé is nothing like that of a functional executive. Choose the correct résumé for your career.

The rule for determining the length of a résumé is this: It must be concise, relevant, and interesting; when it ceases to be relevant and interesting, end it. This leaves a lot of latitude for discretion.

Some professed authorities say a résumé should *never* be longer than three pages; others say the ideal résumé is two pages. Both statements are untrue and based on inexperience.

I helped a man find just the job he wanted when I prepared a five-page résumé for him. How do I know? He told me that as a result of his résumé he was invited to a personal interview. When he arrived in Houston from New York, the decision to hire him was already more than half made. Of course he was a $100,000-a-year executive and a significant achiever. What he had accomplished was a textbook model of finanical management.

Another man had a four-page résumé. It helped him get a vice-presidential position (a step up), involving a transfer from New Jersey to Chicago. How do I know that the résumé was helpful? He has just returned to me after three years to have his résumé updated because the first one was so effective.

But supplying a man or woman of limited experience or achievement with a four- or five-page résumé would be ridiculous—like fitting a size 7 head with a size 7⅝ hat.

In some cases it is easier to write a long résumé than a short one. Therefore, after you have written your first draft, do it over again. Make it as concise as you can while still detailing your achievements clearly.

Additionally, write a *one-page* summary of your résumé in letter form. If you plan to conduct a mail campaign, your background and objectives may suggest that you send a letter instead of a résumé. In any event you can borrow from this summary letter to create a covering letter to accompany your résumé when you circulate it to advertisers, executive search firms, and others.

You might say that a résumé stretches with distance. If you are sending a résumé to a company far from your home base the company will want to know all about you before inviting you to visit for an interview. Teasing the résumé reader with intimations but no proof of grandeur is hardly likely to lead to a personal meeting.

Just as there are few men or women "for all seasons" so there are few résumés, no matter how well written, that satisfy all needs. As an example:

When your job search is carried on primarily through employment agencies, your résumé should be as brief as possible. Some people think brevity means one page. It does not. A new graduate may require just one page. But one can seldom properly get a career on one page.

If your search is directed to higher management levels it may be longer. In the matter of achievers versus nonachievers it is sometimes astonishing to uncover what the former have accomplished. It takes space to explain it and it is certainly worth it.

If your search is confined to an area within easy commuting distance of home base, you can afford a briefer résumé because a personal meeting is uncomplicated for both sides.

Some people have employment objectives in two or three unrelated areas for which they are qualified, each area differing in the way the qualifications are viewed. For example, a psychologist might be qualified for teaching and for private sector personnel work. He will need two different résumés. Similarly, anyone directing a job search in both profit and nonprofit employment sectors will need two résumés.

Law and administration are sometimes equally strong talents in a job seeker. In a job application or a résumé they require two different approaches unless the two functions are combined in a single position.

Therefore, to elicit maximum résumé response it may *sometimes* be necessary to have different résumés according to the people who will read them and the particular job objectives.

For an authoritative treatment of résumé preparation see *Résumé Writing: A Comprehensive How-To-Do-It Guide* by B. E. Bostwick (Wiley, New York), available at bookstores or direct from the publisher.

Example of an Unusual Résumé

CHARLENE RAY
EDITOR

*T*wenty-five years of successful experience as Editorial Director with unusually broad responsibilities embracing three successful magazines with largely female readership; and as Executive Editor, Managing Editor, Features Editor in reverse chronological order; with three different publishers.

*P*ublishers Weekly said: "The most knowledgeable woman's editor in the field." (June 1973)

*M*agazine Guild said: "Miss Ray has helped more aspiring writers than anyone we know." (Jan. 1970)

*M*agazine Writer's Digest said: "Miss Ray has identified her markets and hit them dead center; without question one of the most talented editors in her field." (Nov. 1968)

*C*ompetent in all areas of manuscript selection and purchase, production, control, organization and administration; wide author contacts and excellent reputation for judgment, decisiveness, and creativity.

*P*ossess ability to lead, supervise, train, and gain loyalty and dedication of staff. Oriented to profit.

*S*ensitive to ethical, editorial, and reader needs; capable of coordinating all elements of publishing to gain optimum circulation; and of making quick adjustments if necessary.

*E*mployment
History:
National Publications, New York, N.Y., 1955–1974.
Hillside Publishing Co., New York, N.Y., 1949–1955.
Rex Magazine Co., Topeka, Kans., 1948–1949.

*B*s., Journalism, University of Syracuse, Syracuse, N.Y., 1947.

*P*ersonal data: single, excellent health, no dependents

13

Telephone Campaigns

To use this method to gain interviews you must develop a technique and expect lots of rebuffs. In the job search you will need to grow a thick hide anyway. The rules are:

1 Do some research on the companies you are calling. If possible, try to find a subject of interest to the person you are calling.

2 You have a ready excuse to call if you are following up a letter (a covering letter with résumé or sales letter). You create the opportunity for a personal conversation by preceding your call with a letter.

3 You want to talk with the departmental executive who has the hiring decision for your category: marketing, production, finance, or the appropriate subdivision.

4 If you have not written a letter, use the technique of gaining interest by saying something about yourself of possible value to the person you are calling. Always know exactly what you are going to say before making a call.

5 If possible, use a third person reference (a name familiar to your callee and with the permission of the third person) to gain entry.

6 It is sometimes difficult to get past secretaries. Say that you have something of importance to discuss with the executive you are calling and you must speak to him or her personally. Do *not* say you are looking for a job.

7 By too much persistence on the telephone you can foreclose an opportunity for an interview that might readily have been granted if the way had been paved by a letter.

8 You will find that your telephone technique will improve with practice—and you will get lots of it. For example, you may gain only one or two interviews from 20 calls.

Note: If you want to be a shoe salesman, by all means pick up the telephone and call all the shoe stores in town.

In general the telephone, used for the purpose of soliciting interviews, has some obvious disadvantages.

1 If your campaign is geographically widespread, expense could be a problem.

2 The hours from 12 noon to 2 P.M. are generally nonproductive phoning periods.

3 Differences in time zones require careful planning.

4 Some sections of the country observe regional holidays, or store closings.

5 Calls often cannot be completed because of meetings, days off, or vacations.

14

Broadcast Letters

Broadcast letters are the equal partners of the résumé. They are easier to write after the résumé has been prepared because they epitomize the résumé. They have a special place in the job campaign. The word "broadcast" is widely used to describe one way in which a sales letter can be used. Your sales letter is a "broadcast" letter generalized for mailing to many companies; it is a "sales" letter when you tailor it in order to send it to a specific company as a solicitation for a position, or in answer to an advertisement.

The broadcast letter is a special type of employment application that is widely circulated to top company executives, rather than the personnel department. Its role derives from the fact that many available jobs are never advertised and must be tracked down by mail.

When using the broadcast technique, whether for résumés or for letters, you judge the effectiveness of your mailing by the percentage of response, as would be the case with any mail-order product. A response (inviting you to an interview) of 2% is fair; 15% is excellent.

Broadcasting is one of the quickest and most effective ways of finding a position. Send out at least 100 and preferably as many as 500 broadcast letters. The broadcast letter is used in such cases as the following:

1 Your career level makes it appropriate to by-pass the personnel department.
2 Your talents and experience may have special appeal to a company executive.
3 Your special abilities may cause an executive to employ you now for a position that will actually become available only later.
4 Your qualifications might exactly meet the requirements for a position that the company has been unsuccesfully trying to fill for some time.
5 Your unusual qualifications may be particularly appreciated by a particular executive.

6   You might be well and favorably known at the top executive level of many companies.

7   Your qualifications might lead to an executive reorganization, making a place for you that did not exist until your letter acted as the catalyst to initiate such action.

8   Many top executives, including chief executive officers, like to be made aware of the availability of certain kinds of people.

9   Recruiting an executive by way of a broadcast letter can save a company thousands of dollars in search fees.

The use of a résumé in such cases would nullify your objective—résumés are almost automatically routed to personnel departments. Your broadcast letter might lead to requests for your résumé, which, sent at this point, serves the positive function of satisfying the company's affirmative interest in you.

By using the broadcast letter approach you are not depreciating the personnel department. Many personnel departments do not handle the employment of personnel at higher levels where the subtleties of character and required expertise are difficult to gauge. Employment ideas, amorphous at first, often may be formed only after an interview. Many corporations do not even list employment directors by name in the standard directories.

Caveat: In giant corporations, there is little point in addressing the chairman of the board or the president. The following names are merely illustrative. Some have retired. People like Armand Hammer (Occidental Petroleum), John deButts (A.T.&T.), Harold S. Geneen (I.T.&T.), Thomas A. Murphy (G.M.), Frank T. Cary (IBM), while not necessarily disinterested, have specialists in human relations (personnel) who are top executives in their own right, fully (perhaps better) qualified and authorized to make employment decisions at any level. If your campaign includes such huge companies (as a rule of thumb, over $1 billion), address the vice-president (human relations, human resources, industrial relations, personnel) or the vice-president having responsibility for the corporate area in which you are interested: marketing, production, international, finance, law, administration, and so on.

The rules for writing a superior broadcast letter are these:

1   Start either with (1) an achievement that you think will be interesting to the addressee or (2) your reason for writing. If you use the first alternative follow with the second; if you begin with the second alternative follow with the first.

2 Give examples of other qualifications that show how specially suited you are to provide superior services in your area of expertise. Give four or five carefully chosen examples. Highlight them in short sentences and paragraphs. Leave white space between each point.

3 Follow with a general statement that sums up your qualifications.

4 Provide personal data if favorable—age, marital status, number of children, education.

5 Ask for a personal meeting.

6 Ask for a reply.

You will write a better letter if you have already completed a résumé. Select the material for your letter from your résumé. Your sales letter is a summary of your résumé.

The following is an example of a broadcast or sales letter.

E. Z. RIDER
37 Honda Road
Grand Prix, N.J. 07000

(1)　For most of my career (10 years) I was associated with one company, the last two years as president and general manager and before that as senior vice-president.

(2)　I left that company to enter another as executive vice-president, on the assurance that I could acquire it within three years. I reorganized the production and marketing, reducing costs over 20% and expanding sales by more than 100% within a year and a half, resulting in unprecedented profits. The owner has declined to sell at any reasonable price and I am now seeking another position with a small to medium-size company offering growth and compensation consistent with my abilities.

(3)　Here are some examples of my record.

(4)　—as president of $50 million company developed a new division from zero to more than $10 million over a period of four years, with a pre-tax profit of 20.3%

(5)　—doubled the sales of a second division to $10 million (now grown to $20 million) by stimulating technical progress and introducing new products

(6)　—reorganized marketing strategies of a third division, introduced installment sales, increased volume 63%, reduced ovehead 15%, expanded computer facility, and designed a plan to reduce the impact of fluctuating currency exchange

(7)　—adapted a product, developed for internal use, to meet market needs and added a fourth division to the company that within two years produced $3 million in sales at pre-tax profit of 35%

(8)　These and other achievements may suggest that I am an innovative manager who could be useful to a company seeking management and growth.

(9)　I am married, have three children, attended Cornell University, (B.S., Administrative Engineering) received my M.B.A. from Columbia. Honors include Phi Beta Kappa and Tau Delta Pi.

(10) If there is interest on your part, I would enjoy a personal
(11) meeting. I look forward to the pleasure of hearing from you.

Very truly yours,

(12) Ezekial Z. Rider
Home (201) 000-000
Off. (201) 111-2222

ANALYSIS OF RIDER LETTER

1 The writer starts with his occupational level to help the reader understand immediately who he is. The length of his career suggests his age.

2 He relates an interesting set of circumstances that differentiates him from the usual and at the same time indicates his executive ability. He announces his objective and suggests a compensation level that is readily understood.

3 Leads into examples of his effectiveness.

4, 5, 6, 7 Examples.

8 Makes general statement.

9 Provides personal data.

10 Asks for personal meeting.

11 Asks for reply.

12 Gives telephone numbers.

This writer will gain executive attention. His current level of responsibility establishes immediate rapport with the reader. After a successful career with one company he did what most people would secretly like to do—make plans to have his own business; but it didn't work out. Rider explains concisely what else he has done. He suggests how someone with his background could be useful to the reader. He can afford to understate rather than belabor his excellent educational background.

What does this letter convey?

- General management ability of a high order.
- Experience in all facets of general management, and contributions to each.

- Innovativeness.
- A strong sense of profit motivation.
- A record that suggests value to any company in need of management strength.
- Abilities that were apparent as early as the undergraduate period.
- An age between 36 and 38, inasmuch as "most" of his career is 10 years; graduation with master's degree at 23; two or three years in employment not disclosed; 10 years with one company; almost two years at present company.

This is an actual letter. It resulted in satisfactory employment.

There are many formats. Whichever you choose, you should start your letter with a strong statement about an accomplishment or a capability. Here are some examples:

I made contributions to sales, production, and financial management leading to expansion, lower costs, and better profitability while the chief operating officer of a $50 million corporation.

If you are in need of a senior executive who is accustomed to achieving outstanding results you may be interested in the specifics of the above and additional highlights in my background:

or

With an earlier background as a statistician/data analyst (B.A. and M.B.A. degrees) I have used this ability, as a manager, to reduce costs $2 million and add sales of $12 million within a period of two years, for a $200 million division of a giant company.

If you are in need of a creative marketer who can use data as tools for developing strong forward progress you may be interested in my other accomplishments:

I am experienced in securing a 2000-mile, smuggler-infested coastline along a foreign shore; and in maintaining security for 27 manned outposts in the same area.

If you have need of a security officer I have had training with one of the best educators (U.S.M.C.) and experience under the most rigorous conditions (wartime).

This format is more in the nature of a product sales letter; it is also ideal for a consultant seeking assignments. For letters addressed to top corporate officials I consider it a little abrupt.

ARTHUR MANIASLIP
between Cup and Lip Drives
Bartlett, NJ 07000

Dear Mr. Jones,

I have been employed by two multibillion dollar companies in progressively more important duties over the past 11 years, involving marketing and economics research encompassing the creative interpretation and extrapolation of data resulting in new marketing strategies, sales increases, and cost savings amounting to millions of dollars.

My experience includes projections, financial analysis, cost studies, territory analysis, product and line studies, advertising effectiveness analysis, feasibility studies, computer utilizations and systems, and long-term (25 year) economic planning.

Because my work has been effective for major companies I would now like to have expanded responsibilities and new challenges in a multinational company, which is my reason for writing to you.

Here are some specific examples:

—After conducting a marketing analysis I recommended a new sales approach to drugstores, which has resulted in a 20% increase in retailer inventory turns and a volume increase of $15 million
—Developed a marketing strategy for selected items based on extrapolations of model territories, which resulted in raising our share of market by 10%
—Studied trade promotions, couponing, test market results, and made other evaluations leading to a rescheduling of promotional activities and an annual increase in one line of products by $13 million a year over the past three years
—Recommended a capital improvement program (accepted), improving return on investment by 7%
—Restructured forecasting technique to accomplish an $18 million reduction in inventory with improved product availabilities

I have been widely commended for these achievements, but the present organization does not provide room for the expansion of my responsibilities in the near future.

85

On a personal basis I am 34 years of age, married, with two children, possess an M.B.A. from the Tuck School at Dartmouth, and speak German French, Spanish, Rumanian, and Hungarian.

If my qualifications suggest that I might be of interest to you, I would enjoy a personal meeting.

Your reply will be appreciated.

Sincerely,

GENERAL LETTER APPLICABLE TO MANY PRODUCTS AND MANY CIRCUMSTANCES

I was called upon to work with a reasonably successful pocket-knife manufacturer, as a consultant. A study of the business showed that a number of things were wrong:

- sales confined to one geographical section.
- outmoded displays and packaging.
- a sales force that was nonproductive 40% of the year.
- lack of accurate cost data.
- no budget for sales, advertising, or administration.
- a line of great breadth of which sales of many items were only a few hundred a year.
- product emphasis on items that had ceased to be popular 50 years ago.
- a completely frustrated sales department.
- many employees just hanging on until retirement.

In two years' time, devoting one day a week to these and other problems, I was able to achieve:

- national distribution.
- a reduction of 33% in number of items manufactured.
- a sales increase of 50%, with a 25% increase in profit.
- a new and popular line of knives.
- a new concept in a pocket knife (with patent), of which over 100,000 were sold on the first calls of the salesmen.
- automation of certain production activities.
- budgets for sales, manufacturing, and administration.

Not many companies are in such bad shape. But these achievements illustrate the breadth of my skills.

If your company could use a "total approach" to your problems, with the promise of innovative suggestions to produce higher sales and profits, perhaps I could be useful.

A personal exploratory meeting without obligation would be very welcome.

Your reply is keenly anticipated.

HARRISON D. TODD
14 Old Barrows Road
Ironville, NJ 07111

(1)   Currently, I am Director of Marketing and board member for a
      small ($30 million) chemical company.

(2)   I would like to upgrade my career in a new position offering broader
      opportunity either in marketing or general management. Based on
      my record of effectiveness I can bring dynamic marketing
      performance and decisive management skills to any company with
      a need in these areas.

(3)   To illustrate:

(4)   —for my present company, in a period of less than four years,
      increased volume 150% and provided the earnings base for
      further expansion and plant modernization; I now participate in
      all corporate financial, production, and marketing planning

(5)   —the growth was achieved by means of market analysis, planning,
      raising plant productivity, setting objectives, and creating new
      strategies; and getting out into the field with customers and
      salesmen to explain the new programs, resulting in individual
      orders of as much as $2 million

(6)   —in earlier employment with giant international chemical company,
      progressed from salesman to senior management; tripled regional
      sales in five years to more than $40 million; achieved rank as No. 1
      region in sales and profitability in three successive years

(7)   —trained and recommended 15 individuals for promotion to enlarged
      responsibilities, some of whom are now at top management levels
      in the company

(8)   These are but a few highlights. I have made significant contributions
      in all marketing areas: advertising, sales, promotion, administration;
      in financial areas; investment and acquisitions; and in production
      with cost-cutting innovations for two employers during my career.

(9)   I am 41 years of age, married, have three children, earned an M.B.A.
      at the Wharton School, University of Pennsylvania, and continue my
      education in new techniques and technologies regularly.

88

(10)   If my qualifications meet a need in your company, I'd enjoy a personal meeting.

(11)   I look forward to your reply.

Very truly yours,

(12)   Harrison D. Todd
(201) 000-0000 Home
(212) 000-1111 Office

ANALYSIS OF TODD LETTER

(1)   He says who he is in order to set the tone of his letter.

(2)   Explains what kind of job he is looking for, to let the addressee know at once the reason for the letter.

(3)   Makes a general statement about his accomplishments, which are then supported with examples:

(4)   Example of a very major contribution, resulting in the assignment of broader responsibilities.

(5)   Expresses methods used to achieve the results mentioned, which give credence to his marketing abilities and suggest general management caliber.

(6)   Example of experience in much larger company to give added breadth to his background.

(7)   Example of his leadership ability and his salutary influence on those who worked for him.

(8)   Lists the specific areas in which he has had important experience, showing in more detail his areas of particular competence.

(9)   Provides essential personal data.

(10)   Asks for a personal interview.

(11)   Asks for a reply.

(12)   Provides both home and office telephone numbers for the convenience of his addressee.

I have documented a typical job campaign utilizing a broadcast letter.

Candidate Profile

Functional area   Marketing

Age   50

Geographical employment limitation, Eastern half of U.S.

Employment history

Early career   18 years, very successful

Recent career   12 years, 4–5 job changes; effective
                                    worker but not meeting with great suc-
                                    cess

Nature of Campaign

Number of letters sent   191

Selection of addressees   Careful selection of companies suitable
                                    to subject's background, ranging in size
                                    from $40 million annual sales to large
                                    conglomerates over $1 billion.

(Note: for smaller companies, subject wrote to president or chairman.
For larger companies, he wrote to vice-president, marketing. For giant
companies, he wrote to vice-president, marketing or vice-president, personnel. All letters were addressed to selected individual by name. The
candidate's present business association was not disclosed; this reduced
the number of responses.)

Technical Details

Stationery used   24 lb. bond, monarch size

Color of stationery   White

Method of reproduction   Offset

Heading on letter   Letterhead typed

Method of addressee fill-in   Same typeface as body of letter*

Length of letter   1½ pages

---

* There is an advanced method of photo copying (I am familiar with an Eastman
Kodak copier of this caliber) that is indistinguishable from offset printing and permits
the fill in to match the body of the letter perfectly.

Signature	Personally signed
Replies	Sent to third party to avoid residence disclosure, which would have been a clue to his place of employment.

Responses

Number of replies	101, with 43 different titles which broke down as follows:

> 15 chairman and president
> 18 vice-president
> 25 director of personnel (variously titled)
> 14 manager of professional staffing (and various titles)
> 29 miscellaneous

Number of interviews	6†
Number of job offers	3

Result

Accepted job offer as head of marketing for division of multibillion dollar company

---

† The number of invitations to interview was reduced by the extreme caution of subject in protecting his identity. Nevertheless, his campaign worked. It has been the author's personal experience that mail campaigns are successful in eliciting job offers at least 75% of the time.

15

Sales Letters and Business Proposals

A sales letter is a letter directed to a specific company or to several companies in the same industry outlining the reasons for your special and unusual attractiveness as an employee for those particular companies.

To write such a letter you should be familiar with the company and its needs. You must have a promising idea that, by your best assessment, will have a strong appeal to the addressees.

This letter is a business proposal, with a high level of effectiveness in developing an interview. It is almost never sent to a personnel executive unless it has personnel department application. It is sent to the top functional executive to whose department the idea would apply.

Examples of sales letters appear on the following pages.

LETTER TO COMPANY WITH LARGE STAKE IN DEPARTMENT STORE DISTRIBUTION

If you make a list of department stores according to annual sales and relate your company sales to store size you will probably discover a tremendous variation in sales.

To give you an example, store A in Morristown, NJ did $10,000 per year of our product while a much larger store in Des Moines, IA purchased only $5000 per year. We analyzed the reasons, restructured our sales strategy, and smoothed out these variations to become the dominant force for our product throughout the nation, over a period of 3–4 years.

This is but one example of creative marketing, which I provided for my company. I could list 20 more equally effective projects that I have accomplished. I could do the same quality of work for you.

If you would like to grow faster, increase your profits and possibly become the major factor in your industry, it is highly probable that I can help you toward these objectives.

If this is the kind of thinking you are interested in, let's meet for an exploratory discussion.

Sincerely,

LETTER TO MANUFACTURER (ANY PRODUCT COULD BE SUBSTITUTED, DEPENDING ON YOUR EXPERIENCE.)

Hedge, grass, pruning, and lopping shears (hand operated) make up a line of cutting tools recognized as a product group. Their sale was highly seasonal, concentrated in the spring months. I studied this line and discovered geographical preferences. I found that consumers were influenced by what professionals used. I discovered that we, as manufacturers, were hidebound in our designs as well as our price structure. By a study of horticulture I learned that pruning in much of the United States should be done in the fall and not the spring. I recognized that our marketing department had become overawed by the advent of power tools.

Without burdening you with details, when these facts and others were properly assimilated, it changed the whole concept of our marketing strategy, leading to our ultimate complete dominance of the market and not less than a 15% increase in unit sales each year.

This is the kind of leadership and analysis that I can bring to any line of products.

If such achievements would be of interest to your company I'd welcome a personal meeting.

I look forward to your reply,

Sincerely,

LETTER TO A CONSUMER PRODUCTS COMPANY WITH DISTRIBUTION AMONG HARDWARE, HOUSEWARES, AND DEPARTMENT STORES, AND MASS MERCHANDISERS

A few years ago I made a study of our sales (consumer products) by individual product. We manufactured 250 numbers with sales ranging from a few thousand to several hundred thousand of each. I found that our sales fell into patterns according to end use. These end uses were distinctive, although our sales strategy and our tradition, as well as our salesmen and their customers tended to blur these distinctions.

I created a personality for each of seven numbers and developed a comprehensive presentation and a national advertising program. The result was orders for these seven numbers over a period of six months equal to more than our entire year's sales of 250 numbers and many times the annual sales of the seven numbers.

This is but one of the many ideas I provided for my company to give it the position of owning a 75% share of market nationally.

There is a good chance that I could help your company in a similar fashion.

If you are interested, let's talk about it.

Very truly yours,

A "PIPE DREAM" LETTER THAT DISPLAYS THE ELEMENTS OF A GOOD JOB PRESENTATION THAT WOULD GAIN A BIG RESPONSE

Dear Mr. Smith,

Two years ago I sent the following letter to CAB Communications, the nation's sixth largest national television network:

Watching television nearly a year ago I saw a program called "The $1.98 Beauty Contest." Subsequently I watched "The Gong Show," "Laverne and Shirley," and a so-called sit-com and was appalled at myself for wasting time on such programs. Nevertheless, I decided to watch selected programs regularly for a couple of weeks. I checked these programs against the weekly ratings lists and discovered that the ones I liked least were those that were rated the highest. This presented me with a problem. Was I so out of touch with current taste that I needed to remake my ideas, my attitudes, my basic philosophy?

I decided to do my own testing: I had a circle of 200 friends and business associates and a group of 1000 employees. I solicited their cooperation in keeping a record of their television-watching habits over a period of six months. The sample was exactly 1016 people of different denominations, races, ages, and interests, but all located in New Hampshire.

I used my company computer to analyze the results. Now, six months later, I have a pattern. **Do you know, that pattern provides a picture that is completely at variance with the Nelson reports on which you rely and as a result of which you spend tens of millions of dollars?**

You are being misled. I would like to show you my data.

Needless to say, I was invited to a meeting with the chiefs of CAB. This ultimately led to the establishment of a new network in the Northeast now earning, from only 17 cities, a net profit of $370,000 with a return on net worth of 39%. I am sure you are familiar with the dramatic record, which was so widely reported. The stock has multiplied 16 times since the corporation, New Data Communications, was formed. We have accomplished a revolution in television. All my friends are millionaires and all my former employees have retired. Nonetheless, I am not accepted by the television industry as a whole.

The corporation is off and running, however, and I am now looking for something new to do; I have lots of other ideas.

Would you like to talk to me, and possibly open up areas of mutual interest?

Sincerely,

The conclusions to be drawn from this letter are the following:

1 Things are happening in every industry that are wrong, or wasteful, or misdirected, or poorly accomplished. This applies to automobiles, advertising, food, petroleum, publishing, pharmaceuticals—any industry you can name. If you are smart enough, you can identify corporate errors and capitalize on them.

2 Markets are segmented. One doesn't have to be nationally oriented or even relate to all kinds of people to be successful.

3 Brief but intelligently conducted surveys will often disclose aberrations that even people steeped in their own businesses aren't aware of.

4 Companies will create openings for individuals with ideas.

5 Widely accepted data are not always true, or are true only within certain limits. One has to know the objectives and the methodology of polls and surveys to determine the exact nature of their validity.

Mr. James Eastland, V.P. Finance,
Equitable Prudential Co.
1000 Third Avenue
Chicago, IL 10020

Dear Mr. Eastland:

One of the greatest opportunities existing today for the enhancement of return on investment (and capital gains) lies in real estate.

I have been in this business for seven years as instructor, salesman, appraiser, analyst—most recently as an associate with a prestigious real estate consulting firm working with "Fortune 1000" clients.

In my present position I have become expert in restructuring all the components of a real estate income statement to estimate the market value of income-producing properties for the purposes of investment, divestment, or use.

I have been able to identify opportunities that have been put to use with considerable success by such companies and institutions as General Motors, A.T.&T., I.T.&T., Koger Properties, Prudential Insurance Co., Yale University, Texaco, 245 Park Avenue, Loews, and many others.

My methods include the following studies:
— physical description, underlying fees, air and subsurface rights
— lease analyses (terms, tax, and escalation liabilities; caps)
— debt structure, costs, discounted cash flow analyses (I do my own computer programming for this purpose), yields
— demographics, trends, projections, comparisons

In addition to the careful and precise exposure of value for all kinds of real estate I have had special experience in the analysis of regional shopping centers.

My value would relate to companies with large pension or other funds to invest, for which I could provide reliable analysis and creativity in the identification of real estate investment opportunities to produce optimum yields.

I have both J.D. and B.A. degrees. Age 34, married.

If this background is of interest to your company I would enjoy a personal meeting.

Sincerely,

98

Mr. Richard S. Kaley, Chairman
Columbia Broadcasting System, Inc.
Rockefeller Center
New York, NY

Dear Mr. Kaley:

While **listening** to television recently, I was struck by the misuse of the English language by performers, in commercials, and even by the newscaster.

I am probably oversensitive because in the matter of pronunciation I have what is known in musical terms as perfect pitch. The nuances of pronunciation are my vocation and my hobby.

Although I can hardly add 2 + 2 I am fluent in seven languages including French, Spanish, Portuguese, Italian, German, and Russian, speaking each like a native. This naturally gives me a great advantage in pronunciation because I am able to use the subtle tongue and voice box changes that characterize languages other than English.

It has occurred to me that CBS (I am not pointing a finger at you; I prefer to watch CBS-TV) could well use a language arbiter to assure that all who speak under your jurisdiction use proper English. You have at least this kind of an obligation to listeners who perhaps among their families and friends seldom hear English properly spoken. Furthermore, CBS would come to be preferred by a large segment of the more discriminating audience.

Words like premiere, robust, adult, junta, and a hundred others come to mind as consistently mispronounced. You might well ask, by whose standards? I submit there is room for difference of opinion. I am talking only about **vulgar** or **uneducated** mispronunciation.

I am an assistant professor of English at Columbia University and have written extensively on English usage and phonetics. I have been published by Times Books, McGraw-Hill, and several educational publishers.

You would be doing a great public service and satisfying a personal ambition by appointing me to a new position in your organization (or if there is now such a position, it is inadequately filled), as Director of Language Usage.

I would appreciate your consideration of this idea and your response.

Very truly yours,

Mr. John Wiley Mason, Chairman
General Auto Corporation
Feneral Power Park
Detroit, MI

Dear Mr. Mason:

I am a businessman and a writer, a graduate economist, and a student of government with experience as follows:

1975–Present, Executive Assistant to Senior Vice-President, Automobile Oil Corp., where I am partly responsible for the widely acclaimed institutional advertising campaign directed toward a better understanding of the energy industry and U. S. and world economies.

1970–1975, Chief Executive Officer of a small durable goods company, which I built from $2 million annual sales to $10 million. I retain a 20% stock interest.

1965–1970, Deputy Assistant to the Chief of Government Regulations, Department of Energy and Transportation, Washington, D.C.

1963–1965, Research Analyst, Ford Foundation.

My education is as follows:
Ph.D., Government, Stanford University, 1964
M.B.A., Harvard Graduate School of Business Administration, 1962
B.A., Economics, University of Chicago, 1960
     Phi Beta Kappa, Magna cum laude

My experience has made me an enthusiastic advocate of free private enterprise. I believe that major American businesses must be even more forceful in presenting themselves understandably to the public and to the government. I am convinced that business can not only retain but expand its influence on the U. S. economy with salutary long- and short-term results on the living standards of the American people and, by extension, to the living standards of the world. In other words, I believe in the expansion of the quality of life through the resources of American business.

I want to be a part of and a leader in this progress. My position with Automobile Oil Co. is safe and interesting. However, I want to expand my area of influence with a more diversified company, or a group of such companies. My company knows of my plans. My work is not academic; it

100

influences profits affirmatively with a multiplying effect. I am enclosing some press releases relating to my present activities.

If your company feels that my services would be of value I'd welcome a chance for a personal meeting.

Sincerely,

UNUSUAL APPROACHES

Most top executives will listen with great interest to sound ideas that would contribute to the profitability of their business.

Just as the market for products is a segmented one, so is the market for people. There are so many places to which you can apply for work nationally that a different approach can be made to groups of potential employers. Consider the following:

Humor

Although most executives will be turned off by humor, some might be attracted by it. It is only necessary to get one response that turns out to be the one you want.

Frankness

"I am an ex-convict; I am 62 years old; I have lost all my money in the stock market and must continue to work; I am handicapped; my career has been unsuccessful to date for reasons that may be my own fault; I have special talents of use to a limited number of companies."

Aggressiveness

"You need me more than I need you (describe why); I know your business like the palm of my hand; I can create a new area of business for you."

These are not conventional approaches, but one of them might work with somebody. Try the conventional approaches first—and then try a few unconventional ones.

All of these methods described have been tested, and all work. However, no one method works for all people all the time. One of the most successful systems for gaining interviews is the mailing of résumés or letters to a list of companies. But some people will do extensive mailings and get no responses while others will receive invitations to interviews ranging from 1% to 8% (or even more) of those addressed. Sometimes a mailing will fail one time, and work well for you the next. Why this great variation in response? The reasons are many: badly expressed letters or résumés; inadequate background for the job sought; poor selection of addressees; hard luck; wrong timing; downturn in economic climate; oversupply in a particular field or industry. What works effectively for Smith doesn't work for Jones.

Because this is true it points up the necessity to utilize an assortment of methods, and to use each properly until you find the ones that work best for you. *You cannot give up.* You try and then, if necessary, you try again . . . and again . . . and again.

Another example: for some individuals, knowing the right people is golden; for others, dross. You increase effectiveness by the multiplication of methods.

Another Consideration

There is another facet to consider, which is tangential to the job search but important in career planning. It is going into business for yourself. Some individuals by temperament, ambition, outlook, age, or other characteristics are better suited to be their own boss than to work for others. The same kind of self-analysis is necessary as in preparing for a job search in which you will be working for someone else.

In many opportunities to be in your own business you will still need to show qualifications that give assurance of success. This is true of franchises and businesses in which you are an independent contractor, as in real estate sales, or where you provide free-lance services.

There are plenty of books on this subject, some merely promotional in character, others sound. Probably the best guide to book selection is to rely on the reputation of the publisher or author. Book advertising that suggests that you can become financially independent in a few weeks is usually a rip-off. About half of all new business ventures fail, usually for lack of capital, but also for two other reasons: the business is not viable; the owner is not capable.

Mr. William Lynch, Managing Director
Kellogg, Lynch & Spencer
2 Wall Street
New York, NY 10005

Dear Mr. Lynch:

Subject: Concept

I have been associated with Infometrics since January 1975 as a securities analyst. This is a small financial advisory service handling about $250 million in investments. The company adopted the idea of indexing portfolios a couple of years ago. My studies tell me that this is an incompetent way to handle investments.

I have developed a new system, using 20 measurements of corporate statistics to identify stocks with superior growth potentials. Most of these securities are not found in the Dow-Jones list or even the New York Stock Exchange broad list of companies used for their daily stock movement measurement.

Using these criteria I have made phantom investments (and some real ones) in various groups of stocks over the past three years to test my theory. In some instances I have dumped as many as 50 companies out of 100 within six months after acquiring them because they did not meet my system measurements (for example, starting dividend payments).

Here is my record for three years (Century Theory):

	Dow-Jones	NYSE 500	Century Theory
1977	+5%	+6%	+30%
1978	−4	−2	+35%
1979	−6	−3	+60%

A little luck in including some takeover stocks among my selections served to send the 1979 results beyond normal expectations.

I would be interested in showing you exactly how my system works, and if you like it, to become associated with your company with an opportunity to put this program into action under your auspices.

103

I could establish my own fund, but to do so would take more capital than I can conveniently accumulate, and also require me to reduce my standard of living for several years, which I am unwilling to do.

If this is of interest to you, please phone me to set up an appointment at your convenience.

Very truly yours,

16

Your Scrapbook

Even if you are not the subject of important publicity, keep a scrapbook of any releases in which your name is mentioned:

"*Davy Jones* announced that the strike at Breezy Corners was settled."

"Other speakers were *Davy Jones*, Sam Orea, and Gaspy Salmon."

"*Davy Jones* has accepted the captaincy of the Industrial Division of the United Way drive for funds starting October 1."

"*Davy Jones* will head up the reorganized squad of the Lemon Mountain Volunteer Ambulance Service."

"*Davy Jones* has been elected a member of the Milltown Shade Tree Commission."

These reports are individually insignificant. Taken together, however, they begin to be impressive because they signify leadership qualities. They can be part of an interesting letter to solicit interviews.

Articles about you in newspapers or the trade press or reports of speeches you have made can be direct or indirect ways to elicit interviews: direct if accompanied by a letter of solicitation; indirect if mailed for the general information of the addressee.

Assuming that this material is both business-related and complimentary, it provides a way of measuring you if you are seeking an interview, or a subtle method of placing yourself in the consciousness of potentially important individuals.

Here are two different approaches:

I am sending you the enclosed reprint (article, speech) because it is representative of my thinking on the subject. Inasmuch as the subject is one of importance to executives (within the industry or generally), I thought you might be interested in my point of view. I am desirous of making a change from my present company. If you think a personal meeting could be valuable I would look forward to talking with you.

Alternatively:

In the event that you missed this report (about article, speech), I am enclosing a reprint. The subject is one that is currently of considerable importance to executives in our industry. I am continuing my research to try to find a definitive and economic answer to all the problems involved. If you have any ideas, I'd be glad to explore them with you.

This is only the general idea. Such a letter should be specific with respect to the subject, which is a measure of its importance and what you hope to accomplish.

17

Theses and Dissertations

In the scientific community, as well as in certain professions (teaching, particularly), these works can be quite valuable to indicate the nature of your research, its validity, and your ability to express yourself. In the business sector it is more difficult to use them effectively. However, in many instances if the subjects have been intelligently chosen, the central ideas can be used to create a letter or initiate a conversation.

Here are some of the elements that corporate executives deal with every day: management methods (management by objective, by exception, etc.), marketing and financial strategies, organization, personnel, government regulations, pricing, inventory control, environment, unions, research, invention, health, safety, compensation, and so on.

If you have chosen well in the selection of your thesis or dissertation topic, you may have developed ideas that are useful or even novel. At least you have acquired a set of data with which you are more familiar than anyone else. You can use these ideas and conclusions both as a basis for conversations and for letters leading to interviews. The usefulness of these literary efforts usually diminishes, of course, with the passage of time.

Under some special circumstances the circulation of entire theses or dissertations to prospective employers can gain useful interviews.

18

Public Relations

Cyril Badger announces his resignation from Ladd & Bowater Advertising Inc., to open a new agency specializing in packaged consumer products. Mr. Badger has been Vice-President, Creative Services, since 1974 and is credited with the strategy that has brought Supersoap from fifth to second position in market share in a period of two years. He will be joined by Ms. Sally Taylor, Vice-President of Stout and Rubicund and also by his long-time associate at Ladd & Bowater, Simon Blyth. It is rumored that he has already signed Supersoap.

This and related kinds of publicity appear regularly in the business sections of leading newspapers, financial newspapers, trade magazines, business magazines, and other periodicals. They range from in-depth interviews of leading executives or profiles to announcements of changes in responsibilties. "John Smith will succeed Henry James as Chairman and Chief Executive Officer of Newtech Electronics, effective October 30, 19—."

Some of these announcements are instigated by editors looking for news; some by public relations executives; some by the subjects themselves.

"(Almost) any publicity is better than no publicity."

Public relations can be used in myriad ways, directly and indirectly, to gain interviews. Reprint distribution is obvious.

Some people are perverse and even publicity that is adverse by most standards will be looked upon favorably by a few. Note the number of inefficient public servants who receive job offers upon terminating their government duties. This goes back to the dictum "Publication of your availability for a job is the *sine qua non* of any job search."

Always encourage your company to release information about you to the print media even if it is only the announcement of a promotion. If you have the kind of position that warrants it, get your name and title listed in directories.

People can only be impressed by you if they know you or about you. Awareness of you makes the creating of interviews easier.

19

Write a Book

Authors become recognized authorities in their fields when their books are published. The mention of such publication in a letter seeking an interview will open a door when other methods fail.

Books have been the way to jobs, fame, and fortune for thousands including researchers, professors, lawyers, scientists, real estate developers, investment advisers, managers, accountants—and many people whose career choices ordinarily would not seem to promise so much.

20

Responding by Telephone

If a telephone response is invited, take advantage of the suggestion in preference to writing.

Prepare in advance by writing what you want to say, so that you will be fluent in your conversation.

If a telephone response is not invited but you can get the name and telephone number of the invidual involved in the recruiting process, use the telephone to get information about the job, over and above what has been said in the advertisement. Utilize this information to write a better covering letter or résumé. The more you know about the specifics the better you can respond; by making a better response you give yourself better odds for gaining a personal interview.

21

Personnel Changes

The better business newspapers report changes in personnel, promotions, and appointments. If the companies involved are related to your background, there may be reorganizations occurring that open opportunities to you. Make it a practice to read these changes. Analyze them for possible relevance to you.

This happened to Milford Haven:

The press reported the sudden firing of the chairman of the board of a "Fortune 500" company by the board of directors. In the business community it was a much discussed event. Mr. Haven was the vice-president of another large company, unhappy in his position because a couple of years earlier he had been passed over when a new president had been selected.

He knew a member of the board of directors of the Fortune 500 company, phoned him, expressed an interest in possibly joining that company. He was interviewed by a selection committee and was chosen to be president of the subject company with the promise that if things worked out as hoped he would become chairman in two years.

Everything had happened so fast that executive search firms had not had a chance to go into action, and by his alertness and decisiveness Mr. Haven had taken a step to rectify his possibly fading career. This can happen at any organizational level if one is alert to news releases.

22

Corporate Problems

Magazines like *Fortune, Forbes, Business Week,* and others constantly write about corporate problems and victories. Read these articles with an eye to any personal implications. When a company is in trouble you might have an idea that would be pertinent or a job background that is particularly suitable. If you can save money for a corporation, provide wanted expertise, increase sales, suggest product improvements, or re-organize, you have an asset that is readily convertible into a job. You cannot know about such opportunities unless you read these and similar magazines regularly.

If you know someone in the company, telephone. If you don't compose a letter explaining your unique qualifications or special knowledge.

This happened to Simon Lugrue:

Mr. Lugrue worked for the No. 3 company among the national dis-tributors of bananas, pineapples, and other exotic fruits grown outside the continental United States. With headquarters in Florida, he was the manager of a plantation and distribution point and traveled extensively to find new customers. He learned the weaknesses of his larger com-petitors. He had been instrumental in increasing share of market by a significant percentage. Mr. Lugrue felt that his company had not ex-tended adequate recognition to him, either by title or through compen-sation, for what he had done. When he read in *Fortune* magazine that the largest company in the industry was having management problems, he wrote a letter to the chairman of the board indicating his firsthand knowledge of the reasons for the loss of market share and the low profit-ability of that company.

He was invited to a meeting and after a series of discussions, was offered the position of president.

23

Earnings Figures

Corporate earnings figures are regularly reported in the financial press. Earnings show the company temperature—healthy or sick.

Read earnings figures. If you have a cure for poor earnings, you are just what the doctor ordered

If earnings are good the company may be expanding at such a rate that personnel recruiting is necessary.

Mr. Jetster knew the answer.

Odel Jetster worked for Borealis Airlines as Junior Vice-President. He had a good friend, Edward Rugged, who had retired a couple of years before as Senior Vice-President of Ether Airlines. The two friends often discussed the problems of the airlines: routes, the cost of fuel, regulation versus deregulation, and other matters affecting profitability.

From these discussions and his own observations Odel came to the conclusion that two major problems affecting profits were overstaffing and poor maintenance. With the aid of his friend Edward he made an analysis of the personnel of the two airlines. He discovered that Ether spent over $150,000 a year for the care of plants in its executive offices; that its operating headquarters should be in Atlanta instead of Newark; that there were three vice-presidents for every one needed; that the fleet was only 64% operational at any one time due to slow overhaul. Putting this and more together Odel identified over $60 million of potential savings for Ether at a time when it was losing $5 million a month.

Odel made a presentation to Ether and was appointed Vice-President, Operations, at double his salary with Borealis.

24

Investment or Partnership Offers

Advertisements of this kind are usually run by new ventures, entrepreneurially minded individuals, or companies needing money or specialized assistance.

A follow-up by you if the ad is appropriate to your background might lead to an interesting opportunity or give you an idea.

See the "Business Opportunities" section of major newspapers.

EXAMPLE

An advertiser needed additional capital in his metal-working business. Bill Clay, who had just separated from a company in the hand tools industry, saw the ad, telephoned the advertiser, and made an appointment to visit.

He looked over the plant and equipment and evaluated the progressive presses and dies, power cutters, annealing furnace, high-speed drilling machines, and other equipment with which he was very familiar. He also knew that some companies in his industry needed extra production at certain times of the year that they frequently could not get, and that there were government contracts let out to less qualified manufacturers than this one.

Bill Clay saw an opportunity here; he made calls on some companies he knew about to assess the possibility of getting orders. He also phoned a friend at the General Services Administration (G.S.A) to see what contracts might be available for bidding. He discovered that many G.S.A. contractors were slowing up on delivery and that this government procurement agency would welcome new suppliers.

Armed with this information, Bill was able to enter into a limited partnership with the owner who had inserted the advertisement, and get a satisfactory line of credit from his own bank.

25

"Businesses for Sale" Opportunities

Businesses for sale sometimes can be rewarding for a curious inquirer. You might turn up a chance to go into business for yourself advantageously.

Here are three situations of which I am personally aware:

- A business was offered for sale, and was purchased for two times annual earnings. The deal was so good the job seeker decided to use up his resources to buy it and is happily running the business. Instead of a few bosses he has a constantly increasing number of bosses—his customers.
- A business was offered for sale. The buyer was able to negotiate purchase by paying out of earnings. It was advantageous because he increased earnings. This is like getting a job.
- A business was offered for sale. The seller lied about the potential. The buyer lost his entire investment.

26

Employment Wanted Newspaper Advertising

Employers react with little enthusiasm to "Employment Wanted" advertising by a job candidate.

Nevertheless, employers do acknowledge it as a method by which they sometimes recruit. The effectiveness of such advertising seems to be related to its creativity. We relate these successful experiences:

An advertisement in *Time* magazine resulted in employment for one advertiser. It was expensive, but worth it in this case because it reached his prospective employer.

An advertiser ran an ad in *The New York Times,* along with his picture. It was an unusual tactic—and it resulted in employment.

An advertiser ran a half-page ad in his industry trade magazine. It got him an unusual amount of atttention, and some kidding. It also got him a job.

27

Community Activities

Participating in fund drives for charities seems rather far removed from getting interviews. However, here is a succession of events:

Jim Stanley lived down the block from Thor Larsen. Thor was older but they were good friends of long standing, and played bridge together every week. Thor was involved with the local hospital and acted as a captain in the annual drive for funds every year. He asked Jim if he would take some file cards and call on seven people in the neighborhood. Jim agreed. He learned a little about the hospital and made the calls; he collected 100% above the quota assigned. It wasn't too difficult because previous gifts had been nominal and few of the people he called on had ever been told about the needs of the hospital.

The next year Jim was asked to be a captain; as such, he was responsible for recruiting 10 people to call on their neighbors. Jim got a group of friends together for coffee and dessert one evening, told them he wanted them to help him in the annual drive, told them something about the problems, costs, and advantages of the hospital and most agreed to go along. He held weekly meetings to monitor results.

As the group neared its quota, Jim's enthusiasm increased and he turned the fund raising into a game. His team was surprisingly successful. Over a period of a couple of years, Jim was given larger responsibilities. The hospital joined the United Fund. Jim became a member of the board of directors of both the hospital and the United Fund. In this capacity he met a great many important local businessmen. He became a member of the budget committee of the United Fund, which investigates the money needs and resources of the charitable institutions making up the group. He devised an organized plan for making the budget investigations, which replaced the informal methods that had hitherto prevailed. Many of the institutions objected because they did not want to disclose the extent of their endowments. Jim was sure of his ground and explained his theory to the board. It would mean fund approvals of greater amounts for some institutions and cuts for others. There was a great uproar, but the logic of the theory was irrefutable. Jim's plan was adopted.

In the meantime Jim wanted to change jobs. He mentioned his desire for a change to the members of the Board, just in passing. Much to his surprise, five of them said, in effect, "Stop in and see me in my office sometime at your convenience. I might have some suggestions for you."

The "suggestions" turned into three job offers. Jim is now vice-president of a major insurance company.

Constructive community activities include school, library and museum, fairs, flower shows, shade tree commissions, church, youth work, recreation, board of education, and many other involvements. Most people who get involved only go through the motions. Those who are dedicated and can lend a degree of excellence to their participation often have the same kind of thing happen to them that happened to Jim.

28

Making Speeches

College and university business schools always need interesting outside speakers. Trade group secretaries are always seeking someone who can express a point of view of general membership interest at meetings and conventions.

If you are asked to speak and you are qualified, accept. You will become known and regarded favorably throughout your industry. If you wish, you can get all the interviews you want as a result of this kind of activity.

Here is a very simple but typical example. Mendel Milkey was chosen to head up the entertainment committee for the annual convention of the National Hardware Manufacturers Association. He pursued the same general program as his predecessor—with a few minor innovations.

He explained the events that were to be held at the first formal meeting of the membership on the opening morning at the convention. Everyone was there. Consequently, everyone knew who Mendel Milkey was.

From that beginning Mendel was elected a member of the board of directors, became widely known throughout the association, and was invited to an interview and offered a position by a competitor of his employer at a much higher salary.

29

Run for Local Political Office

If you live in a small community where political service is unpaid and only part time, run for office: town committee, board of education, councilman, tax assessor. You will become widely known. When you are widely known you have a base for generating interviews that is unequaled.

In the village of Milltown, Arne Brinkerhoff ran for town council. There were few candidates and little interest except among his friends. In apathetic voting, he was elected.

At town meetings he showed himself to be sensible, bright, and without any axes to grind. The next year he was elected mayor. During the course of his activities he met many prominent men and women. One day, out of the blue, he was offered the presidency of a large pharmaceutical company.

Why? The mere title "mayor," even of a small village, carries connotations that expanded his importance and provided a character that other candidates, despite perhaps greater competence, did not possess.

Possibly he was able to exhibit greater talents as a mayor than he could have as a middle management employee. Or maybe a new status was conferred on him in the highly visible political job.

30

Serve on Boards

To be asked to serve on a board is usually an honor, but sometimes it turns into a disaster. Board membership is epidemic. Individuals who serve on one board are often asked to serve on another, and then another and another. Abel Carter, vice-president of a small company, was asked to serve on a cemetery board without recompense. He accepted, found it stimulating, mainly because the leadership was somewhat stodgy and he had fun infusing some life into it. Oddly, there were several important people serving also, who had similar but minority ideas. He was soon invited to serve on the board of a manufacturing company, for which he did receive reimbursement. As time passed he had more invitations than he could accept.

Tilden Williams was a fairly important executive. He became a board member of a medium-size company. The president resigned under pressure. There seemed no one suitable to take over. The selection committee sounded out Tilden. He accepted the job, later becoming chief executive officer. Under his guidance the company moved from a volume of $200 million a year to become a major conglomerate.

Arthur Ashton was a broker. He was asked to sit on the board of an insurance company. Both the chairman and the president died. Arthur was asked to become president and accepted. He says of himself, "I take no great credit. I always seemed to be in the right place at the right time."

Moral: Members of boards of directors seldom seem to be out of a job.

31

Religious Affiliations

There is a commonality of interests among people who belong to the same house of worship or the same denomination.

If religion is a part of your life program, your fellow worshipers will be interested in your employment plans. This is true within your community and also among congregations geographically far removed.

For example, if you go to another city or small town to seek work, touch base with a house or houses of worship.

Without drawing any other similarity, the same condition applies to such international business clubs as Rotary. An enthusiastic Rotarian, for example, will give preference in job selection to another Rotarian, all other factors being equal.

An individual who is known to attend the same church or temple as a job interviewer gains a slight edge. A slight edge could make the difference.

32

Support a Political Candidate

Millions of people gain jobs because they have political connections. Party support and loyalty are highly regarded. Note how many politicians, after losing an election, for example, are given jobs by the party faithful. Nephews, nieces, wives, brothers, third cousins once removed, find jobs easily. Sometimes one doesn't even have to appear at a workplace. Knowing the right person, whether in business or politics, is a major way of getting an interview and a job, except that in politics the interview may be unimportant.

Join a political group.

Eyeing 1980, Carter's aides throw more appointments to Democrats who might help him in primary contests. Seats on the U.S. delegation to the UN go to a leading party fund raiser in Maryland and a New Hampshire campaign contributor. A civil-rights leader is named to the Federal Council on Aging. A son of the late Chicago Mayor Daley lands a spot on an advisory council. (*Wall Street Journal,* September 21, 1979)

33

Conduct a Public Relations Caper

A group of college graduate job seekers organized a run along a predetermined route, stopping on the way at company employment offices in Manhattan, and released the news to the press. The press picked it up and the episode was given extensive coverage.

It is probable that few of these imaginative candidates failed to get interviews.

Climbing up buildings or church steeples, jumping off a bridge, giving out quarters with a résumé at an exclusive business luncheon club, handing out résumés on a street corner to likely looking executives— all these are methods that people have used to gain attention for themselves and get interviews, or job offers.

This method is only for a few hardy souls.

34

Hire a Public Relations Firm

In the upper-income bracket you can employ your own public relations firm, paid tax-free out of your own pocket. What can result from this? News releases, profiles, business stories, announcements, and all kinds of items in the print media, which, more frequently than one might think, welcome interesting information.

In some instances, public relations executives can influence appointments to boards of directors.

Many business leaders gain attention without seeking it. If you are not one of those, let a public relations firm do some work for you if you can afford it. Done subtly, it can be very advantageous.

The president of a company I once worked for unabashedly used the services of our public relations firm to further his own interests. The p.r. firm had many city contacts and suggested this man—I'll call him Likerd Liss—to many corporations as a prospective board member. As a result he was invited to join and accepted service on several boards. The companies involved were unaware of the Machiavellian machinations involved in Liss's campaign.

35

Trade Association Activities

Every industry has its own trade association, and sometimes several. Associations encompass a broad range of activities and each requires a committee. Demonstrate your interest, get a committee appointment, and do what is required. If you do it well you will be noticed.

Getting interviews comes from being known.

Simon Manfred became the chairman of the admissions committee of a small power tool association. He spoke briefly about admissions at every meeting. Actually he spoke the same words at each meeting, varied only by the names of the companies being introduced for membership.

He became widely known in the group. He was tapped for the presidency of a much larger company. He showed qualities of self-assurance, even-handedness, unflappability, and a certain small-town dignity. Apparently people liked these traits.

36

Writing for Publication

Most executives with upper-level responsibilities become aware of ideas, practices, or needs that would be of interest to other executives. If you have developed a plan that was successful for your company, and are not bound by secrecy, write about it.

For example: a method of motivating workers, a new compensation program, an advertising concept, a better forecasting tool, useful yardsticks in sales improvement, meeting techniques—any of these ideas and thousands more can be expressed interestingly.

Those who read your articles may be impressed and will be willing to talk to you. This applies whether you are employed or unemployed.

Milton Bradshaw was asked to participate on a committee of manufacturers sponsoring, along with a group of wholesalers, an educational program for these same wholesalers. The objective was to improve the very low profitability level of the wholesalers in this particular industry, which was declining to lower levels each year and was then running at an average of 2.04% on sales.

After the program was established, one of its features was to assign an identifying number to every product handled, identifying it by generic type regardless of price, weight, efficiency, brand, or any other quality. Many of the managers did not understand the concept, or didn't listen to the explanation.

Milton Bradshaw did. Several executives asked him to express his opinion. He did. He was the sales manager of a small company. He was subsequently asked to occupy the same post in a much larger company— one that had asked his opinion.

37

Letters to the Editor

Letters to the editor that are published and say something unique or important, or are impressively written can be reprinted and used as a method to gain interviews.

One young man, an enthusiastic and expert skier living in Hawaii, wrote to *Business Week* about the fun of skiing on Mauna Loa. Many people did not even know that there was skiing in Hawaii. The letter writer received many replies expressing interest.

One individual made it a point to meet the letter writer, a professor at the University of Hawaii, on a visit there and was so impressed by his knowledge of global geography that he offered him a position as an editor and project researcher on the staff of his national magazine.

38

Meeting Customers and Clients

Even if you are not in a position to have personal associations with clients or customers, make it a point, whenever possible, to meet them. Perhaps you can do your job better if you are aware of customers' or clients' problems. This could be true with respect to sales, credit, data, service, product quality, shipping, or any other business area.

Get to be known.

Vadic Petaschinsky was the customer service manager of a company with heavy interests in distribution through department stores. The company sales manager had just closed a deal with J. L. Dayton Company of Detroit, one of the nation's largest department stores, involving 16 feet of counter space on the main floor and an elaborate display installation. Extensive advertising plans were completed for the opening day, which coincided with a strongly promoted store fashion show.

The company received a frantic telephone call from the vice-president of Dayton—the display was not right! Vadic was rushed to Detroit by plane. He worked in the store until 3 A.M. on the night preceding the opening, doing carpentry, reassembling units, repositioning products, and finally getting the display ready.

The store vice-president was so impressed that he offered Vadic a job in operations, a much better job than the one he held. Vadic accepted. I have followed this man's career. He is now Vice-President, Operations at Dayton.

39

Relocation

Employers may be willing to talk to you if they know you are willing to relocate. If you believe that you cannot leave your home ground, you are likely to miss many golden opportunities.

Do not place a handicap on your selection by your unwillingness to relocate. If getting a job is more important than geographical location, be willing to go anyplace where opportunity exists. There may be no job for you near your present home, while the perfect position may be available in Dodge City, Iowa.

Keep an eye on population changes. Thus between April 1, 1970 and July 1, 1975 the population has been increasing faster than the national average of 4.8% in the South and the West, but slower than the national average in New York, New Jersey, Pennsylvania, Michigan, Ohio, and other industrialized northern states, with New York and Rhode Island actually losing population. The largest percentage population increases occurred in the following states:

		Population gain*
Arizona	25.3%	449,000
Florida	23.0%	1,566,000
Nevada	21.1%	103,000
Alaska	16.3%	49,000
Idaho	14.9%	107,000
Colorado	14.7%	324,000
Utah	13.8%	147,000
New Mexico	12.7%	130,000
Wyoming	12.5%	42,000
Hawaii	12.3%	95,000
New Hampshire	10.9%	80,000
Arkansas	10.0%	193,000

* All the data on population given here are from U.S. Census Bureau, *Population Estimates and Projections*, Series P-25, No. 615, December 12, 1975.

Not all of the large percentage increases indicate significantly larger populations, hence greater opportunities, but they do indicate trends. The following states show less significant changes in population:

		Population gain
Oregon	9.4%	196,000
Texas	9.3%	1,038,000
South Carolina	8.8%	227,000
Montana	7.7%	54,000
Georgia	7.4%	738,000
North Carolina	7.2%	365,000
Tennessee	6.7%	262,000
Maine	6.6%	61,000
California	6.1%	1,214,000

40

Working As a Consultant

If you are out of work and knowledgeable in some area of business, offer yourself as a consultant while you are looking for a job. Your consultancy may lead to a permanent position, or at the least will help you to get along during the job search.

Victor Seidel, a production manager for a nationally known consumer products company (electrical), lost his job after a 23-year career with the same company. He had been an effective executive, but his company was acquired by a much larger one that believed in restaffing.

He circulated his availability as a consultant to several hundred companies. Immediate high income was not imperative. He became associated with a group of new business developers and his expertise proved valuable.

The product was an oil additive that unlike so many on the market had demonstrable merit.

A corporation was formed. Victor became an officer. The company is now prospering.

41

Aiming at Selected Companies

After some study, you have determined that you would like to live in or around Kansas City, Missouri because it offers a location and a quality of life that you would like, as well as growing business opportunities. Of course it could be Houston of Phoenix or Stamford or San Diego or New York or anywhere else. Look up businesses suitable to your expertise or experience in Kansas City. Refer to directories for this information (see Interview Method 102, "Using Lists").

Select three to six companies having special appeal to you and study these businesses by reference to annual reports, and visits to bankers, brokers, and the local Chamber of Commerce. Determine their profitability, problems, competition, and reputations. Call on retailers, distributors, or others handling their products. Get market information: rate of sale, packaging, quality, complaints, policy, pricing, selling effectiveness. Talk to employees of the company. Learn what they think about the company and about employee turnover; pick up whatever information you can. Try to find people among school friends, religious associations, athletic clubs, and business organizations who can either directly or indirectly provide you with information. Organize the information. Develop ideas.

Decide with whom in the companies you would most like to talk: chairman, president, departmental vice-president, or some other executive. Approach that executive by telephone or by letter. If through personal acquaintances you can get an introduction, so much the better. Tell him or her you have been interested in this company and would like to learn something about it, and ask for a few minutes for informal discussion. You are not looking for a job. You are interested in the industry. If an interview is granted, use the opportunity to express some of the ideas you have resulting from your company research. Ask about the problems of the company.

After such an interview, added to your own research, you should be able to develop some ideas that would be of possible value to the company. When you have organized your presentation with great care, ask for another meeting on the basis that you have an interesting idea to discuss. Job offers sometimes are made after putting programs of this kind into operation. Meetings are relaxed because you are not, ostensibly, looking for a job and your interviewer is not under pressure to make an evaluation for employment.

Here is an example of a letter that might have been written following a meeting initiated as an informal discussion of mutual interests, rather than as a job interview meeting.

Dear Mr. Bartholomew,

Thank you for the opportunity to sit down with you two weeks ago and explore interesting aspects of the hand tools business. I have been interested in this area for many years, for special reasons, although my experience has been in consumer soft goods. It was good of you to give me your sales figures broken down by territory and states.

Just as an exercise for my own edification, I have used Department of Commerce figures on sales in the hand tools classification, expressed in percentages by states. Using your figures for New Jersey, your best state, as 100%, I have extrapolated what each state would do in sales if it were as well handled as New Jersey. Calculating your potential sales in this way and allowing for certain distributional aberrations of which I am aware, I find that **you have a potential national market 327% greater than your present sales.** I know you sense this, but these figures prove it.

Furthermore, using Florida as an example, where your sales of circular saws are greater than all the rest of the U.S. together, because of special circumstances (a retiree with an encyclopedic knowledge of saws, selling direct to retailers), an opportunity of huge dimensions is uncovered.

You might be interested in studying these figures. I have also noted some of the steps that would need to be taken to move toward such objectives. My experience in marketing tells me they would not be easily accomplished, and very possibly would need a dedicated five-year program.

I have had personal experience in implementing programs of this kind, and know with certainty that their achievement is possible.

I will phone you in a few days. I will be glad to find the time for an in-depth discussion of these findings if you are interested.

Once again, thank you for the opportunity to learn more about your business. My hobby is business analysis.

Kindest personal regards,

Note: There are many small businesses—and this was one (sales about $1.8 million)—that reward their owners and a few others with substantial incomes. I know of one company president operating a business of only $750,000 annual sales who paid himself $125,000 a year in 1965. The comforts of operating in a small niche often settle into an inertia that conceals substantial opportunity well within reach. These smaller company executives are often easier to reach and more expansive than their opposite numbers in giant companies.

The following is a hypothetical but possible response and denouement after a second meeting has been held. The writer of the letter was George Buckminster. The owner of the company was John Bartholomew. By the end of the second meeting George and John are on a first-name basis. About 7 o'clock one evening, a few days after the second meeting took place, the telephone rang at George's home and the following conversation took place.

Hello George, this is John Bartholomew.

Hello John, how are you? How nice to hear from you.

George, I've been thinking about our last conversation. It seems to me that your approach to, and understanding of my business are very sound. How would you like to come to work for me?

Thank you very much, John. You take me completely by surprise. Of course, I'd like to work for someone like you and I can see great opportunities, but I have had my eye on a position with a larger company. Frankly, I see myself in a bigger area than the hand tools business. Your suggestion is very flattering, but I'm not sure I'd be the right fit for you.

Look George, I'd be willing to give you a five-year contract, a good salary, and a share of the profits if growth transpires, as well as stock options.

As I said, John, I am highly complimented and as an individual, I can't think of anyone I'd rather work for than you. My objective, however, has been entirely different. I'll tell you what. Let me think about this for a few days, and discuss it with my wife.

Take some time. But you've opened up some thoughts that I have to resolve. Just let me hear from you again within the next two weeks, one way or the other.

Thank you for calling, John. I'll be in touch.

42

Questionnaires and Surveys

Prepare a questionnaire about some aspect of a business or institution about which clarification as to methods and procedures would be useful as an addition to general knowledge, or as a basis for an article.

Telephone or write executives whose jobs are related to your line of inquiry and try to get an appointment to gain answers to your questions. One such effort in 10 or 20 will lead to a job interview.

Paul Mendelsohn noticed that many cartons became damaged in shipment and that frequently the name of the shipping company was not shown, except on a small label.

He tracked down cartons in his own large warehouse. He found:

- Damaged merchandise.
- Unidentifiable cartons.
- Missing merchandise.
- Cartons that were too small.
- Cartons that were too heavy.
- Merchandise lacking reshippable packaging.
- That there was some, if not great, advertising value in well marked cartons.

He conferred with other manufacturers and accumulated much data. He analyzed his findings and discovered that there were losses being borne by shippers and insurance companies that ran into millions of dollars.

He was asked to present his findings at a national manufacturers convention. His ideas caught on and became a national issue in trade magazines around the country. What do you think happened to him? He was invited to become the warehouse manager of the largest consumer goods manufacturer in the U.S.

43

Volunteer

Be ready to accept or volunteer for any assignment to write, speak, or chair a committee, even if you are not reimbursed, in order to gain exposure.

For example: a trade association circulated a questionnaire asking how it might be of more value to its members. I can tell you from personal experience that responses to such a question are amazingly few. One individual took the trouble to answer this question in detail, including some very good and constructive ideas. The result was election to to the Board of Trustees and subsequent wide exposure in the industry, which led to several job offers. One such offer was accepted and the man described is now president of an important company in that industry.

44

Research

In your spare time, research an area of interest and write about it, trying to hit upon a novel approach that would gain the attention of other executives.

Examples are: management techniques, Nielsen reports, media language, advertising, product development, productivity, investment, retail merchandising, retail departmental management, industry problems, techniques for dealing with unions.

Use your report as a platform from which to step into meetings with selected executives.

45

Write a Newsletter

If you are in advertising or public relations or accounting or executive search or securities or many other fields and you foresee that you might be looking for a new job in the future, write a monthly or bimonthly newsletter. Send it to a list of important executives.

In these occupations there are always new concepts, interpretations, regulations, and other happenings that are worth reporting. Many people do not have time for business reading and appreciate getting important information in capsule form.

If you write, produce, and distribute your newsletter intelligently, you will find friends among executives who could be of value to you.

For example, one British friend of mine opened his own advertising agency but had too few clients. He had family in England and one client there, so he visited about four times a year. He studied business conditions there and on the Continent, which led to a quarterly newsletter that contained ideas and observations of value to multinational corporations. Soon he was gaining new clients and was finally absorbed by a giant agency on very good terms, while retaining his own autonomy of operation.

46

Luncheon Invitations

From time to time, make it a point to have luncheon with someone whom
you do not know really well but have reason to think might have interests in common with you.

Helen Hammond met Eva Eden at a party and discovered that they
both had gone to Skidmore College but at different times.

They had luncheon together one day at Helen's suggestion. Eva worked
for Evon Cosmetics. Helen had an administrative position in a bank and
was dissatisfied. It developed, during the course of the conversation,
that there was an opening at Evon for someone with Helen's interests.
Eva arranged an appointment and Helen was offered a position that
she accepted.

47

New Acquaintances

When you make a new acquaintance at a party, on the golf course, at a resort, on a ship, playing tennis—whenever you make a new acquaintance—find out what business that person is in.

I know a banker who does this consistently. It annoys some people— but not too many. She is a very successful banker. As a banker she knows she has information useful to many people. Individuals to whom she is helpful are in turn helpful in giving her personal or commercial accounts.

You too, whatever your business, have useful information.

Exchange it!

48

Conducting Seminars

If invited to, conduct seminars on subjects for which you are qualified. Do it without charge, if necessary. You will make many important contacts.

William Blackstone was invited to participate in an A.M.A. seminar on wholesaling. He was considered an expert in this field because of his extensive consulting assignments and earlier experience in wholesaling in a family-owned business in Canada.

He had developed some ideas of his own, among them that most wholesalers suffered from poor inventory turnover, from too great a rigidity in profit margins, and from overemphasis on self-generated capital, which often squeezed them for cash and reduced their ability to utilize business techniques long since adopted by other industries.

Bill elaborated on these themes at his seminar. His "students," all either wholesaler executives or owners, were so impressed that he was employed as a consultant to set up an educational program for the industry in the entire Northeast.

49

Working Without Pay

If you are out of work and an attractive opportunity presents itself, take a job without pay to prove your effectiveness. Positions of this kind have often led to productive and satisfying employment.

Preston Smith had been fired from his job with a hand tool company for reasons having largely to do with a personality conflict with the president of the company. One of his good friends and a customer of his former employer was a manufacturer of hand tools of very specialized kinds, made in small quantities. Customers included the upholstery trade and some hardware wholesalers. Preston asked his manufacturer friend, Jim White, if he could work for him, without salary, to see if he could come up with any new ideas. If he did produce anything profitable, the agreement was that Preston would get paid a commission.

After a few weeks Preston developed an idea for a consumer upholstery kit. He had samples made and presented the idea to half a dozen wholesalers. They bought it. The product turned into a good seller. Preston then selected a couple of tools, one a hammer, all beautifully made and more costly than similar tools carried by most wholesalers. He developed packaging and display, and combined them with a longer discount structure that was being widely demanded by wholesalers.

The wholesalers liked Preston's products and his pricing. Jim White was convinced and offered him a job, which has gradually become more important. He is now sales manager in a company that had existed profitably for over 100 years without one.

50

Be a Joiner

Organizations exist so that individuals with common interests can exchange points of view.

Join, selectively, luncheon clubs, local business organizations, the advertising club, the sales executives' club, and others.

Casual meetings sometimes result in fascinating opportunities.

51

Nonprofit Employment Assistance

The "Forty Plus Club" is a not-for-profit organization that helps unemployed individuals over 40 years of age to gain interviews and jobs.

One example is the Sales Manpower Foundation, a division of the Sales Executives Club of New York. This organization maintains a nationwide résumé file of sales and marketing people currently seeking new assignments.

52

Job Exchanges

Specialty magazines and associations—engineering and chemistry come immediately to mind—have job exchange services and regularly list openings available in their fields.

Be sure to make use of any that operate in your field.

53

Using Cartoons

You can sometimes add effectiveness to a letter or presentation by using an appropriate cartoon from a magazine or newspaper.

54

Using Samples

If your occupation leads itself to the idea, provide a sample of something you have made or done: a dress, shawl, booklet, advertisement, gift idea, recipe, and so on, and write or telephone for an appointment to show it.

Sally Scrimshaw's hobby was weaving on a hand loom. She learned at school and at home. She had a good eye for color and design. She made up some scarves, skirts, shawls, and other items in designs of her own imagination.

Sally took her samples to designers, fashion centers, department store buyers, and textile manufacturers. She became a designer for a famous textile manufacturer.

Sally had talent but no one would have known, had she not aggressively promoted her samples.

55

Telegrams

If you have something very important to say to a prospective employer use a telegram or mailgram to gain attention and action. Follow up with a telephone call.

If one is self-important, one sees every incident as significant. If one is employed by an important organization, that importance transfers itself to the individual. Thus if you receive an invitation to subscribe to *Time* magazine, the letter you receive, written at a lower middle-management level, is so compelling on first reading that you wonder if you can be an intelligent member of society without reading *Time*. If you put the letter away for a few days, the urgency of the decision diminishes. It is so with many other things. What other people think is advantageous to you (where it involves their own advantage) is seldom so, in the final analysis. Nevertheless, there are ways of expressing oneself that suggest thoughts, ideas, or information of great moment. You can create that urgency in a Mailgram or telegram.

Mr. Frost, President of Penny Candy Company, received the following Mailgram:

> Have important information re consistent competitors plan to undermine reputation of your company. Your Sparklies alleged to cause gum disease. Dealers around Kokomo are returning their stacks of Sparklies to their distributors. Feel you should know full details in my possession. Will phone you tomorrow for meeting.
>
> Signed: Fred Smith

Most things of this kind turn out to be so many grains of sand on a beach. However, there *are* situations that are truly important. If you know about one, use a Mailgram.

It is notable also that some executives are highly responsive to approaches of this kind, just as some executives like to answer their own
telephones rather than have their calls screened. In digging for interviews you never know what might work; you know only that some procedures work more frequently, and are more widely accepted than
others.

56

Career Advisers

Many people do not know how to conduct a job search for themselves and would prefer not to learn. Their belief is that their time on the job is more important to them than looking for a job, even though a new position is of great importance.

Others feel inadequate in their ability to write or talk about themselves.

Under these circumstances, employ a qualified professional to write about you, guide you in interview planning, and conduct a job search for you.

There are many quacks in this field. Select the person or group you decide to work with, with great care.

"Blue ribbon" corporations employ specialists like this for their "outplacement"; that is, when important executives are separated from their employment, their companies help them find new, and sometimes better jobs.

Many top executives have successfully employed career specialists to find a new position. Fees range from $800 to $6000 or more, depending on how much work has to be done.

57

Third-Party Endorsements

If people of importance agree to write a letter of introduction for you to an individual with hiring authority or influence for the job you would like to have, you are almost guaranteed an interview. *Equipped with the support of such individuals, this third-party endorsement is the single most important route to interviews—and often jobs.*

People who are little known generally sometimes have inordinate prestige at high levels, to such an extent that if a request is made to meet a certain person, that request cannot be turned down. Such people have such great prestige because they do not use their influence idly, or in support of unqualified people. The scale, of course, runs down from this level all the way to the point at which some dubious sponsorship would be harmful instead of helpful. On balance, you benefit by having a third person say something good about you.

To give some examples:

A senator, congressman, lawyer, accountant, general, or corporate or investment executive could know something about another executive that indicates that the employment of the candidate would be beneficial if there is an opening.

A buyer would be aware of the excellence of a salesman who calls on him or her.

A company would always know the key executives working for a competitor.

A professor is able to assess those who have been in his class.

An advertising agency account executive can measure the competence of a corporate marketing director, and a marketing director, conversely, can measure the efficacy of an advertising agency.

A corporate director knows the ability of fellow directors.

Bankers are in a special position to know and rate the management of the companies they do business with.

Third-party endorsements are not more widely used than they are because many people just do not have that kind of wide acquaintanceship. If this were not so all hiring would be done by word of mouth, which, of course, is not so.

152

SAMPLE LETTER

Mr. J. Russell Stout, Vice President
Colgate Cyanamid Co., Inc.
Colgate Park
Bright Bond, NY 08967

Dear Mr. Stout,

I retired last year as vice-president of the Empire Bank, but continue my association as a consultant to the bank and as a member of the board of directors. One of my assignments has been upgrading our manpower development department. In this capacity I have had an opportunity to meet a large number of promising executives both in and out of this company.

I have also become aware of your own change in marketing strategy from product to market departmentalization, with which, incidentally, I agree.

The purpose of this letter is to tell you about a young man who has had substantial success in his own company, but now faces an uncertain future because of his company's acquisition by a much larger one.

He has had a ten-year career since gaining his M.B.A. degree at Stanford and is widely recognized in his industry (chemicals). In the last couple of years he has been credited with increasing share of market for his company's major line of proprietaries by more than 50%, and at an increased R.O.I. He also introduced the same marketing moves in which you are currently involved.

It occurred to me that such a man might be of interest to you. If so, call me, or drop me a line and I'll set up a meeting. Needless to say, I have no personal or financial involvement in this other than an interest in seeing a highly talented individual find the right spot for his career development.

Kindest regards,

58

Appearance of Written Presentations

When an interview is solicited by a written presentation of some kind, excellence in the appearance of that writing, entirely apart from content, can favorably influence your selection for an interview.

Good paper, quality reproduction, use of a good typewriter, attractive spacing and paragraphing, freedom from corrections and smudges—all these factors contribute to the impact of your correspondence.

Do not underestimate appearance.

Over half of the résumés and letters that pass through interviewers' hands are poorly typed and reproduced and therefore far less effective as a basis for interview selection than a neatly typed résumé of someone who is not necessarily a better candidate.

LETTERHEADS

Your personal printed letterhead can be an advantage in the appraisal of your letter, as compared with a heading that is merely typed in.

In order of attractiveness:

1 Engraved.
2 Raised (thermograph).
3 Flat.

Do not use a company letterhead unless it is a company you own.

AUTOMATIC ELECTRIC TYPEWRITERS

Letters typed on an automatic electric typewriter give the impression of an individually typed letter. It is flattering to an addressee to think that he or she is the only recipient of a personalized letter.

Advantage—the personal touch.
Disadvantage—the expense.

Most executives today are sophisticated enough to know that automatic electric typewriters exist and are not impressed that a job candidate has spent $1.50 on a letter rather than 10 or 20 cents.

On balance, however, there is a plus in this method of reproduction.

INDIVIDUALLY TYPEWRITTEN LETTERS

In your most important correspondence, in which you are writing only one or a few letters to find the job you want, have the letters individually typed. There is no substitute for the personal and complimentary atmosphere this creates.

STATIONERY

In any correspondence relating to a job search, use only quality paper. Good stationery enhances the appearance and tone of your writing.

The use of heavy, high-quality, off-white, Tiffany-grade stationery for letters (with engraved letterhead) or résumés will almost of itself demand reading and, if the candidate's qualifications meet the need, assure an interview. The use of such stationery is unusual enough to gain special attention and carries connotations of personal pride, good taste, achievement, and assurance. This is applicable only to jobs sought at a high organizational level.

59

Positioning Yourself for a Better Job

You may change jobs satisfactorily by getting a better job in your present company; this is sometimes better than changing companies. It is a good precept for every employed person that he or she learn the requirements of the boss's job, and the one beyond that, and the one beyond that, and so on. This can be done by observation and by reference to formal job descriptions. Some people exceed the limits of a job description in their job execution, others do less. It is more common that performance is less rather than greater, so that generally there are opportunities for the alert. A survey* of 1708 senior managers in Fortune 500 companies (over 55% earned from $76,000 to $150,000 a year) elicited responses from over 500, stating that among the traits that enhance executive success the three most important are:

Concern for results	73.7%
Integrity	66.3%
Desire for responsibility	57.8%

From a different point of view, the three factors most influential in decisions to change positions are:

Increased responsibility	44.0%
Increased challenge	42.0%
Better compensation	31.9%

It is no coincidence that "responsibility" is prominent in both responses. The search for additional responsibility is a key characteristic of the upwardly mobile manager. It should be noted that one reason for job separation is that a job becomes too comfortable and the occupant loses the impulse to continuously seek improvement of job administration. Creativity, enthusiasm, and diligence sometimes wane.

* Korn/Ferry International's Executive Profile: A Survey of Corporate Leaders. Korn/ Ferry is a leading executive search firm.

Managers need to review their objectives, decisions, and work habits on a regular basis to be sure that they are assigning the same or greater value to their work as earlier in their careers, and that they stay abreast of technological and other changes.

One way to avoid the onset of boredom in a familiar occupation is to play the game of managing the next higher position or any position to which you aspire, no matter what the level. If, for example, you work for one of the "Big 3" automakers, what would you do if you had the responsibility for running the company? Despite their reputation for superior management it might be easier than you think to improve upon it.

Why are foreign cars making such inroads on American manufacturers? Why are dealerships in such bad repute with respect to service? Why are cars built to become obsolete? Is it really necessary to have yearly model changes? Is the trunk of a car the best place for luggage? Why aren't gas tanks made large enough to eliminate irritating road stops for gas over relatively short distances? Why can't the doors of two-door cars be made less cumbersome, with perhaps entrance to the back from a rear door rather than by climbing over a front seat? Why can't someone make a car eliminating all the fancy embellishments—a really trimmed-down car that would be inexpensive to buy and cheap to operate? Why can't bumpers be made to resist bumps at 10 or 15 miles an hour instead of five miles an hour? Why doesn't some automaker buy the best tire company, so it could equip its cars with the best tires? And so on.

What would be your recommendations?

60

Third-Party Solicitations

If you are in a sensitive position in which the mere mention of your name in connection with a job feeler would set off repercussions, you may have to use a third-party approach to guard your anonymity.

Should this be necessary, the effectiveness of your search will be unavoidably diminished. This does not mean that it cannot be successful. It does mean that the volume of favorable responses will be less.

If you are fearful that in responding to a blind ad you might be writing to your own employer, draft a résumé under the name of a friend and in that way identify the advertiser.

Here is another procedure: create a résumé or letter that does not divulge your name or identify your employer. Select a friend, acquaintance, or professional service (adviser, for example) to write, sign, and mail a covering letter for you. Enclose the résumé with the covering letter.

The letter should say something like this:

> The subject of the enclosed résumé is a friend who is widely known in his industry and wishes to keep his search for a new position confidential. I have offered to act as a middleman for him.
>
> A reading of the résumé will enable you to decide whether the qualifications described are of interest. If they are, please phone or write me to set up an appointment. If an appointment is offered, my friend will confirm to you directly and identify himself at that time.
>
> There is no compensation or other obligation to me if employment should follow an interview. Thank you in advance for your consideration.

Should the intermediary be an individual of standing, there will naturally be an advantage to you; but it's not necessary that this be so.

61

Follow-Up

If you answer a help wanted advertisement and do not get a reply within two weeks send a letter asking for a response and reiterating your interest. Perhaps you can add another persuasive point at this time that was not included in your first reply.

TELEPHONE FOLLOW-UP

If you have written to a prospective employer and have received no answer, you have an excuse to telephone your addressee. To his secretary you can say, "I wrote to Mr. Smith about a week ago and I want to discuss my letter with him, briefly." To Mr. Smith you can say, "I am calling about the letter I wrote you about a week ago." You will ask if you can meet with him. You will want to know what he thought of the letter. If his company has no openings does he know of a company that might? Could he offer any advice about revising the letter? Not everyone will accept your call or be willing to respond, but your letter has opened the way to a *possible* conversation that would not be available if you had not written at all. You have a beachhead on his attention and you should exploit it.

62

Choosing the Right Approach

For best results in gaining interviews choose the kind of writing most suitable to your circumstances. It may be:

- A résumé.
- A letter.
- A proposal.
- A thesis or dissertation.
- A copy of an article or speech.
- An advertisement.
- Several of the above, each to meet particular conditions.

From reading this book you should know how to select the writing approach best for you under any circumstances.

63

Business Proposal

You might know a particular industry well enough to form an idea about a new department, a new distribution channel, or a new product.

One job candidate wrote a 60-page presentation suggesting a new department to expand the influence of a company in a new area. He addressed it to six companies, received invitations to a personal meeting from five of them, and was employed by one—although not in the capacity described in his business proposal.

The presentation was worth the effort because it elicited interviews with companies he was interested in, and resulted in a job he enjoys.

64

End Run

The following was reported to me by a friend:

Some years ago I was invited to interview for a position as editor for a book publishing company. My interviewer, Bob Edwards, talked to me for a while and finally said, 'We also have an opening for a publisher in one of our divisions. I think that it would be better for you to apply for that job. Mr. Allen is conducting those interviews. I'll set it up for you.'

I knew that at the time I was not qualified for the position of publisher. I suspected that Bob Edwards had someone in mind to whom he wanted to give the editorial job, and would like to see me disqualify myself by shooting for the higher position. I found out the name of my interviewer's boss, phoned him, and said: 'Mr. McSorren, I have just had an interview with Mr. Edwards, to fill the editorial position you have open. Mr. Edwards suggested that I apply for the position of publisher, which is also open. I know I am not qualified for this job, and so does Mr. Edwards. I fail to understand why Mr. Edwards is steering me away from the editorial job. I am a damned good editor. I could do an exceptional job for your company in this position, based on my record with Rowe & Morrow. Could I meet with you for a few minutes?'

Mr. McSorren agreed to the meeting. In the end Mr. McSorren interviewed all the editorial candidates and selected me for the position. It developed that Bob Edwards had a personal friend he was trying to promote for the job and hoped that he could finesse me out of contention.

This is an example of an end run to get the "right" interview instead of the "wrong" one.

65

Copy-Test Your Writing

If you have sent correspondence of one kind or another to potential employers and are not getting invitations to come for an interview, analyze your writing for detrimental areas and *rewrite*. Copy-test whatever you write.

One person wrote a résumé in which the word "unexceptionable" was used in a description of his qualities. The word has entirely favorable meanings; "unimpeachable" is one synonym. Nevertheless, the subject received no replies to his résumé. He wrote another résumé, deleting the word "unexceptionable," and received 10 invitations to interviews from a mailing of 100 résumés. People had misconstrued the meaning of "unexceptionable," taking it to mean "unexceptional."

As in advertising, sometimes a single word makes the difference between success and failure.

66

Salary Disclosure

In general, don't disclose your salary history or expectation in résumés or letters.

In answering ads specifically asking for this information you may write your expected income range, with pen and ink on your covering letter, but if you have a strong résumé or covering letter, omit it.

If you are assured of your worth and would not change jobs except for a large increase in your present salary you may disclose what you expect.

Never give your salary history unless you have enjoyed dramatic increases in a short span of time. Such earnings increases are the best measure of your value to your present employer.

Compensation is highly negotiable and you lose flexibility by advance disclosure. If you are conducting correspondence with an executive search firm, it must know your income range.

Of course this applies only to middle and upper management levels. At the entry level, salary level must be disclosed.

67

Accomplishments

What you have done successfully in your past employment is your strongest weapon both in oral and written communication. Be as forceful as possible in telling what you have done because it is the measure of what you can do in the future.

68

Reason for Leaving Last Job

In any written communication avoid reasons for leaving any past jobs *unless* the reasons are unusually favorable to you.

Reasons for leaving sometimes require overlong explanation or can be downright unfavorable.

69

Consulting and Free-Lancing

The word "consultant" in a résumé as a present occupation for an extended period and after a series of jobs usually indicates that you have been unable to find a job. Avoid the use, if possible.

The phrase "free lance" is also suspect, except where free-lancing is common as in art, journalism, writing, copy editing, and so on.

70

Part-Time Job

Part-time jobs sometimes lead to interviews for full-time employment. A part-time job in sales might disclose that if you worked full-time you could add many times the value of your salary to the company. A part-time accounting job might show that closer attention to costs would more than offset the additional expense of regular full-time employment to your employer.

Ask for an interview to present your recommendations.

EXAMPLE

Richard Nickson answered an ad for a part-time bookkeeper-accountant for a men's clothing retailer. The books really didn't take much time and on several occasions when one of the salesmen was out sick he would fill in. Extra sales help was always needed on Saturdays and holidays and just before Christmas. He applied for a sales job at these peak times, was approved and paid by the hour at slightly above minimum wage. A fringe benefit was a discount on the purchase of clothing.

Richard did well in his selling and finally approached the proprietor with the idea of full-time sales work. He was accepted when another employee moved to a different company.

71

Single or Married

When hiring younger people, employers prefer single women and married men.

Married women are more likely than single women to become pregnant or have parental duties that will affect their job productivity. And although women are moving increasingly into executive positions, it is still more likely for a woman to relocate because her husband's employment requires it than for a man to relocate because his wife has been promoted.

Married men, for several reasons (some spurious), are considered more dependable employees than single men.

72

Outplacement

Executives who are separated from their jobs (fired or displaced) may be able to take advantage of a corporate service being offered increasingly by enlightened employers. The service is called *outplacement*. It has become a specialty of many firms who are paid by the employer to search every avenue to gain reemployment for separated employees.

A good outplacement firm will use all the necessary techniques, such as those described in this book, to find suitable employment for their clients, and the fees are paid by the company.

Many executives who have been separated from their jobs have found even better jobs. Being fired is not necessarily a catastrophe.

73

Discover Poorly Managed Companies

Your broker researches or reads research on hundreds of companies. Ask him or her to give you the names of companies that are badly managed. If your expertise is suitable to aid such companies, prepare a proposal and ask for an interview.

Examples of how such opportunities have been pursued by others can be found among the letters and proposals appearing in the sections on those subjects.

74

Fund Raising

Accept a fund-raising assignment from your college or university. It is a good way to widen your circle of influential acquaintances.

75

Athletic Excellence

Some companies may be interested in you because you excel in certain sports (for example, golf). If a company is hiring a salesman or someone who attends conventions in which a day or two of golf is part of the program, there is some benefit to the company in having a winner or near-winner on its payroll. Of course a golfing talent is not a substitute for work effectiveness, but it can add to your attractiveness and provide an area of special rapport with customers.

Sports excellence at a professional level is obviously useful in public relations, advertising, politics, and some nonprofit work. Witness Joe DiMaggio, Mickey Mantle, Bill Bradley, Bill Russell, and a host of golf and tennis pros. Even if you are not well known, your athletic abilities are an asset and will help you to get interviews.

76

Hobbies

Interesting hobbies lend scope to your personality and show that you are not just a one-dimensional person. Mentioning them in a résumé is constructive and adds to your odds in gaining interviews. A prospective employer whose passion is iceboating will be tempted to "have a little chat" with a candidate who puts it on his résumé.

77

Customer Following

If in the course of your work you have created a group of customers more loyal to you than to your employer, such a following can be of inestimable value to another employer.

In any request for an interview by letter, point out that you have important connections of immediate value to a prospective employer.

People about whom this could be true include brokers; other salesmen; advertising clients; accountants; lawyers; news, weather, and special feature commentators; columnists; bankers; real estate agents; waitresses; and financial advisers.

78

Writing Grants

The words "writing grants" are an idiom for writing a proposal for a grant.

The ability to write an effective proposal, one that will gain interest and then effective action, is an acquired art highly regarded in the nonprofit sector (not that profit doesn't occur in nonprofit activities, if only in the form of a job).

The elements of a good proposal are:

1 Identifying the correct addressee(s).
2 Explaining the need.
3 Outlining the concept.
4 Defining the goals (long-term), and objectives (specific).
5 Detailing the organization.
6 Providing the time frame.
7 Estimating the budget (in comprehensive detail).
8 Summary.

A well-conceived grant proposal will lend a great deal to an interview and, if the proposal is acepted, could lead to one and possibly several jobs.

Writing grants is the nonprofit sector term for a business proposal.

79

Professional Résumé Writing

At the beginning of a career one often does not know what to include in a résumé. At mid-career one may not know what to omit.

If you do not care to learn how to write your own résumé; if you are too busy; if your time is too valuable for such an effort; if you do not write well; if your knowledge of English is deficient; if your experience is outside the United States and different résumé standards apply; if after having written your own résumé you find it lacking—then go to a qualified résumé writer and get professional assistance.

The most difficult hurdle in writing one's own résumé is finding a sense of objectivity about oneself.

80

Pursue Outdoor Activities

Participate in a sport: golf, tennis, squash, softball, soccer, touch football, riding, running, skiing, swimming, platform tennis, handball, and other games. Golf and tennis are the most useful in social and business relationships.

Friendships formed in games are among the closest you can make, and playing games offers many opportunities for expanding acquaintanceships.

81

Be Distinctive

Make yourself different from the crowd. Learn how to be a good conversationalist. Dress better. Drive a distinctive car. Be alive. Use a cigarette holder. Don't always talk to the same people at a party. Seek out new friends and meld them with old friends. When you entertain, do it with style. Form groups for discussion, music, bridge, investment, or your own special interests. Make people glad they know you. When you attend a party, realize that you have an obligation to give something of yourself to help make it a better party.

82

Emphasize Special Attributes

Although it is illegal for employers to discriminate, you may choose to emphasize your special attributes that make you more attractive to a particular employer.

These could be age, sex, race, religion, political leaning, or any of hundreds of factors that might give you a special edge under special conditions.

Soothing Hispanics. Attorney General Civiletti caters to Hispanic-Americans, who used his confirmation hearings to complain of mistreatment. He promises to pick an Hispanic attorney as a special assistant. Civiletti hosts a reception for the Justice Department's Hispanic employes, presents employe awards during Hispanic Heritage Week. (*Wall Street Journal* September 21, 1979)

83

References

Although references are not ordinarily included in a résumé or presented until real interest in you has been demonstrated, some exceptions can be made.

References from famous or widely respected people can be helpful. In the political area, references can be especially valuable; in fact, they can be more important than anything else.

84

Campus Recruiting

Recruiting on campus is a favorite way for many large companies to find entry-level employees. If you are an undergraduate, be sure you participate. Some M.B.A. graduates from the most respected schools receive starting offers of $27,000 to $40,000 a year.

85

Executive Search

If you are fortunate enough to have an executive search firm pursue you, a job interview may result. You will first be screened by the search firm.

The preferred executive search firm is the one that has an assignment from a corporate client to find a particular executive. Some search firms work on speculation, however. In talking with an executive search firm you can be just as curious about the opening involved as the firm can be about you. The give and take can be much more candid than in the usual job interview.

If you are not interested in the job described, suggest the name of a friend or associate who might be. The favor might be reciprocated in connection with a future job that does interest you.

Being on good terms with an executive search firm can lead to other interview opportunities. If you are not currently seeking a new position but think it conceivable that you might be at some future time, send a résumé to a group of them and explain your position. It might lead to a splendid opportunity later on.

Inasmuch as it is unusual for two or more executive search firms to work for the same client, you may send your résumé to as many firms as you wish. Your income level should be a minimum of $35,000 for you to be of interest to the best search firms.

86

Husband/Wife Employment

If you and your spouse both work and you are offered a position far away from your present location, arrange for your spouse to have an interview also. Possibly he or she can be employed by the same company, thus avoiding a family separation, a long commute, or loss of work by the other member of the family.

87

M.B.A. Degree

Having an M.B.A. degree, as applied to business employment, adds to the number of interview opportunities that are going to be offered to you, and possibly to income increments. If there is a way for you to gain this degree without creating undue hardship for you, do so.

A mystique has developed around the magic letters "M.B.A." At this time, 1980, salaries for new graduates are at a median range of $20,000 to $22,000 and as high as $40,000 compared with $13,000 for undergraduate B.B.A.'s. However, the number of M.B.A. graduates has risen from 21,325 in 1970 to an estimated 52,000 in 1980.

Many personnel executives and academic leaders think that a glut of M.B.A. holders is coming. Graduate programs in colleges and universities have proliferated to some 500, while the most sought after graduates continue to be from the top 20 schools such as Harvard, the University of Pennsylvania, the University of Chicago, and Stanford. Only 20% of graduate-level business schools are accredited by the American Association of Collegiate Schools of Business. Many recruiters prefer several years of business experience prior to the earning of the degree. Actually about one-third of all M.B.A. students are part-time students already holding corporate jobs.

The glitter of the M.B.A. may be showing spots of tarnish, but it is still a ticket to a tryout for a preferred part in the play—so long as it is not thought of as an automatic guarantee of a leading role.

88

Open Houses

"Open houses" are used by some companies to attract desirable employees from entry level to executive. These are held in-house after work hours or in motels, days and evenings.

Even resort areas are used in the hope of interesting vacationing executives who might be considering making a change in employment.

89

Job Postings

Many corporations post notices about jobs that are available in other corporate sectors. Giant corporations are so big that it is impossible for every department, division, and subdivision to maintain a cross-reference or career history on each employee.

Better jobs than the one you might now have may be becoming available in the very company in which you now work.

The job posting procedure is an attempt by companies to promote from within.

90

Civil Service

Take a civil service examination. Get your name on the list of available job candidates. Take civil service competitive and promotion examinations as they are announced. Civil service examination dates are regularly posted in post offices and other federal buildings.

91

Over 65

Many people who are retired or of retirement age prefer to continue working. Enjoyment of work, the satisfactions of the work place, authority, inadequate pensions, inflation—all contribute to the fact that an increasing number of people at 65 years of age and older are working or looking for work.

Among the services catering to this group is MatureTemps Inc., a personnel agency that handles part-time employment for older workers. They have offices in major cities, including New York City.

92

Drive a Taxi

The following was excerpted from *Advertising Age* (January 14, 1980).
  Related by a candidate for a job with an advertising agency as copywriter:

> My letters, calls, and portfolios were not getting me a job. I took
> a job driving a taxi, which I equipped with a sign that said, "This
> taxi is being driven by an unemployed advertising copywriter." I
> kept a portfolio of my work with me and a stack of résumés. My
> campaign turned up several free-lance assignments. Three months
> later, a passenger got me an interview with her husband (creative
> director of an agency). I was hired on the spot.

93

Speculative Executive Search

List yourself with executive search firms who work on speculation, as described earlier, or use a professional career counselor to offer you to selected corporations. For example, an executive search firm working on speculation without an assignment or a career counseling firm might present you in this manner:

CANDIDATE NO. 1087

In the course of our work for Fortune 500 clients we have met a young, personable, effective, creative, experienced marketing vice-president who has had a career of 10 years with two leading consumer goods companies.

He has been instrumental in a major way in increasing sales over 50% for each, at the same time lowering the percentage cost of sales. He earned his M.B.A. at the Harvard Graduate School of Business Administration.

His present company has been absorbed by a giant conglomerate and he expects that the new owners will restaff with their own people. He is willing to relocate.

We do not have an assignment at this moment for this executive, but his qualifications are so good that we think you might be interested. If so, please write for complete details without obligation. Refer to client number 1087. Salary requirements in the fifties, plus incentives.

If you use this method of seeking interviews, it will be at your own expense unless the search firm working on speculation is willing to absorb the costs.

A comprehensive national list of executive recruiters, including those who work on speculation, is available for $10 from Consultants News in Fitzwilliam, New Hampshire.

94

Pictorial Representation

If your message is one that can be represented by symbols more effectively than by words, or as a supplement to words, it is now possible through technological advances in photocopying to reproduce graphics inexpensively and in color.

Separate units of art from totally unrelated material can be cut, joined, pasted, made into a collage, or otherwise utilized, to provide a personal presentation limited only by your imagination.

95

Who's Who

If you are writing to an executive who is listed in *Who's Who* or a similar directory, knowing his activities, age, schooling, clubs, home address, interests, and employment history could possibly be helpful in formulating your letter.

This approach is feasible only if you are writing to a limited number of companies. The background of your addressee might spark an idea. Try it.

96

Teasers

You have seen the teaser technique at work in selling books and motion pictures, among other things. The same idea may be effective with employers. Send one letter a day to an executive you want to meet.

DAY ONE

For my present company, I had an idea, arising from data research which I organized and implemented, that resulted in a doubling of annual sales within a period of six months. Perhaps you would be interested in this kind of creative thinking in your company.

DAY TWO

For my present company, I have achieved a 65% share of market over a period of 10 years, at the highest prices in the industry. Possibly the techniques used would be of interest to your company.

DAY THREE

For my present company, by means of a unique merchandise presentation, I have provided over 300 giant retailers with a sales return in excess of $450 per square foot, leading to retail dominance at 25,000 subsidiary retailer counters. Would this kind of market penetration be of interest to you?

DAY FOUR

For my present company, I took one of our former best sellers, which had reached a mature plateau, and opened a brand new market for that product that is larger than the original one. Could you find a place for an individual who can provide this kind of innovation?

DAY FIVE

For my present company, a labor-intensive business, I devised a new automated production technology that promises to lead us to worldwide domination in the industry. I would like to put my imagination to work for you.

DAY SIX

Combine all these elements into one letter that concludes your mailing. Ask for an interview. Ask for a reply. In the first five letters you may disclose your identity, or conceal it until your final letter. Both methods have been used successfully.

97

Valentine

It was early February. An artist seeking a job with an advertising agency sent the agency president a personally developed valentine—clever, attractive, unusual. She was invited to an interview and offered a job.

You may be able to use holidays and anniversaries as a basis for an unusual and timely approach.

98

Dollar-Bill Message

Dear Mr. Burdette,

I am not trying to corrupt you—only to gain your attention long enough to read this brief letter. Please give the enclosed dollar to a child's piggy bank, your favorite newspaper vendor, or favorite charity.

(Go on to explain who you are in a well-phrased letter, expressing your special qualifications for employment.)

99

Charts and Graphs

Use sophisticated charts or graphs to illustrate dramatic sales increases, cost reduction, salary growth, increases in value of company or stock exchange, or other factors suitable for graphic presentation.

This material can supplement a résumé, letter, or other correspondence.

Graphs are based on the following data (000 omitted) :

	1977	1978	1979	1980	1981
Sales growth	$10,000	$13,000	$16,900	$21,970	$28,551
Profit growth	1,200	1,690	2,366	3,295	4,569
Sales cost (%)	15	14	13	12	11
Return on investment (%)	6	8	12	18	24
Income growth	$25	$32.5	$50	$75	$100

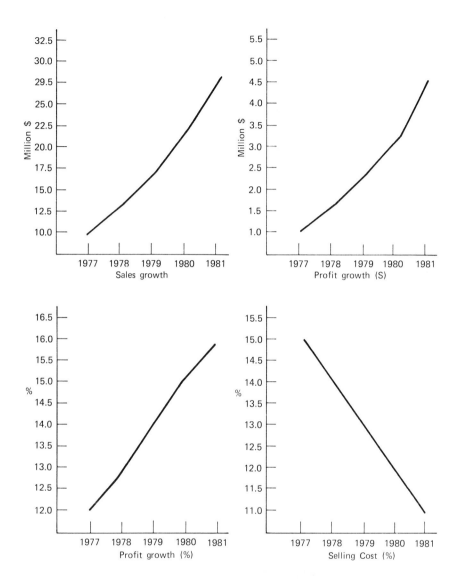

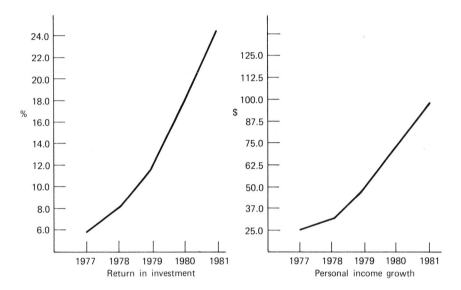

Return in investment

Personal income growth

100

Using the Headlines

If your job is related to investments, use whatever the current state of the market is to illustrate your capacity to make correct decisions.

If you use this approach, your timing must be exquisite.

Kidnappings, bank threats, and the like, in the current news can be the basis for offering security services.

Tight mortgage money can provide the basis for other lending techniques not based on mortgage liens.

It is frequently worthwhile to look at the reverse aspect of any situation. For example, when price cutting (i.e., low profitability) prevails in an industry it may be an opportunity to reverse course and bring out a premium line (such as, blue jeans).

When stocks drop below book value, companies buy up their own stock, if they can afford it, and automatically over the long run increase its per-share value.

If you have sound ideas along these lines that you can apply to companies you're familiar with, you can gain employment.

101

Using the Calendar

The time to look for a job is when you need it, whether it is summer, Christmas week, or any other time. However, to *optimize a job campaign that includes mailings,* use the calendar to identify the best times of the year for attention to you.

The business calendar is shrinking. Out of 365 days only 189 are usually productive in the context of a job search, and this number is probably overstated. It does not include Jewish holidays, Wednesday closings in New England, fishing and hunting days in the Midwest, weekday golf in the South, or holidays like Election Day, Veterans Day, Flag Day, Washington's and Lincoln's birthdays, or the disruptions that occur when the individual states and the federal government fail to concur on the proper date for a given holiday.

Furthermore, traditional two-week vacations have given way to four to six weeks for executives and long-service employers.

The calendar year is an arbitrary measurement. The more typical business year is October 1 to September 30. One works 8 months, until May 31, slows down in June, rests part of July and August, whirls through Labor Day, and recovers from rest and whirling in September, to start October with fresh vigor. It is no accident that the automotive industry model year begins in October.

There is another shorter hiatus in January and February for two weeks, for trips to Florida or skiing country, or for cruises. The business year is further interrupted by conventions, other business travel, directors' meetings, government meetings, and miscellaneous days off. It is no wonder that employment decisions are notoriously slow in the making.

The 189 days have probably shrunk by now to 150 days.

In your job search, in using the mails you should avoid July and August, Christmas week, and Thanksgiving week. Aim at the first five months, the last three weeks of September, the month of October, the first half of the months of November and December. More specifically, try to have your mail delivered on Monday, or better still, Tuesday of the most useful weeks. After a Monday holiday, however, Wednesday and Thursday become the preferred days. Avoid having mail delivered on Friday. Monday is a busy day for diving into accumulated decisions, Tuesday is more relaxed, Friday (TGIF) is a tapering off day when new decisions are seldom made.

Some people are even superstitious about Friday; for example, it is supposed to be a bad day to move into a new home, and of course Friday the 13th is the worst day to do anything! None of this is absolute, of course. It is just giving yourself the edge when it is possible to bend the calendar to your uses.

In correspondence, avoid the shaded days, weeks, and months on the accompanying calendar.

JANUARY								FEBRUARY								MARCH					
S	M	T	W	T	F	S		S	M	T	W	T	F	S		S	M	T	W	T	F	S
	1	2	3	4	5	6						1	2	3						1	2	3
7	8	9	10	11	12	13		4	5	6	7	8	9	10		4	5	6	7	8	9	10
14	15	16	17	18	19	20		11	12	13	14	15	16	17		11	12	13	14	15	16	17
21	22	23	24	25	26	27		18	19	20	21	22	23	24		18	19	20	21	22	23	24
28	29	30	31					25	26	27	28					25	26	27	28	29	30	31

APRIL								MAY								JUNE					
S	M	T	W	T	F	S		S	M	T	W	T	F	S		S	M	T	W	T	F	S
1	2	3	4	5	6	7				1	2	3	4	5							1	2
8	9	10	11	12	13	14		6	7	8	9	10	11	12		3	4	5	6	7	8	9
15	16	17	18	19	20	21		13	14	15	16	17	18	19		10	11	12	13	14	15	16
22	23	24	25	26	27	28		20	21	22	23	24	25	26		17	18	19	20	21	22	23
29	30							27	28	29	30	31				24	25	26	27	28	29	30

JULY								AUGUST								SEPTEMBER					
S	M	T	W	T	F	S		S	M	T	W	T	F	S		S	M	T	W	T	F	S
1	2	3	4	5	6	7					1	2	3	4								1
8	9	10	11	12	13	14		5	6	7	8	9	10	11		2	3	4	5	6	7	8
15	16	17	18	19	20	21		12	13	14	15	16	17	18		9	10	11	12	13	14	15
22	23	24	25	26	27	28		19	20	21	22	23	24	25		16	17	18	19	20	21	22
29	30	31						26	27	28	29	30	31			23	24	25	26	27	28	29
																30						

OCTOBER								NOVEMBER								DECEMBER					
S	M	T	W	T	F	S		S	M	T	W	T	F	S		S	M	T	W	T	F	S
	1	2	3	4	5	6						1	2	3								1
7	8	9	10	11	12	13		4	5	6	7	8	9	10		2	3	4	5	6	7	8
14	15	16	17	18	19	20		11	12	13	14	15	16	17		9	10	11	12	13	14	15
21	22	23	24	25	26	27		18	19	20	21	22	23	24		16	17	18	19	20	21	22
28	29	30	31					25	26	27	28	29	30			23	24	25	26	27	28	29
																30	31					

102

Using Lists

To conduct a job search campaign by mail you need to refer to directories and lists of various kinds to develop your personal mailing list. Your list should be tailored as closely as possible to the kinds of companies, geographical areas, and other characteristics that reflect your personal needs or preferences.

The names and addresses of corporations and organizations and the names of their personnel can be obtained from the following sources, which are found in most libraries:

1 Dun & Bradstreet Million Dollar Directory.
2 Telephone directory *Yellow Pages* (company and organization names and addresses only).
3 Standard & Poor's *Register of Corporations, Directors, and Executives.*
4 State industrial directories.
5 Industry associations (almost all major industry classifications have one).
6 *Thomas' Register of American Manufacturers.*
7 *Martindale-Hubbell Law Directory.*
8 *Moody's Handbook of Common Stocks.*
9 *The Value Line Investment Survey* (published by Arnold Bernhard & Co., Inc.).
10 *Rand McNally Bankers International Directory.*
11 *Fortune's* annual supplement listing the 1000 largest corporations (no individual executive names) and other listings.
12 *Forbes's* annual list of 2500 corporations (no individual executive names).
13 *Hardware Age Directory* (published by Chilton Co., Radnor, Pa.).
14 *Pharmaceutical Handbook.*
15 *The Standard Advertising Register.*
16 American Management Associations publications (such as Executive Search Firms).

17 *The Literary Marketplace.*
18 *MacRae's Blue Book.*
19 *Standard Rate and Data Service.*
20 *United States Government Organizational Manual.*
21 Trade magazines.
22 *Directory of Foundations in Massachusetts.*
23 *College Placement Annuals.*
24 Association of Consulting Management Engineers (New York City).
25 The *Wall Street Journal* daily list of corporate operating reports.

Standard & Poor's Register of Corporations, Directors, and Executives contains an alphabetical listing of the names of about 35,000 corporations; 300,000 officers, directors, and principals; and 70,000 officers, directors, trustees, and partners. *Fortune* magazine annually lists the 1000 largest industrial corporations as well as the largest financial institutions and the largest overseas corporations. *Stores,* a National Retail Merchants Association publication, annually lists, by volume, the leading department stores. *Forbes Magazine* has an annual listing of 2500 major companies.

If you prepare your own list of companies to write to, make use of the S.I.C. (Standard Industrial Classification) numbers to identify a company's business. Many companies have multiple S.I.C. numbers. The first two digits of the four-digit S.I.C. number show the major industrial group to which a company belongs:

01 to 09 Agriculture, forestry, fishing.

10 to 14 Mining.

15 to 17 Construction.

20 to 39 Manufacturing.

40 to 49 Transportation, communications, utilities.

50 to 59 Wholesale and retail.

60 to 68 Finance, insurance, real estate.

The last two digits classify each company more closely; for example, 3172 and 3199 refer to leather goods and 2844 to cosmetics. A cross-reference to the main body of the register (Standard & Poor's, for example) will then give you the address and size of the company and names of executives. Many big companies are unexpectedly missing, as are some divisions resulting from mergers. Most lists, as distinguished from directories, do not include location, area code, names of executives, and products. Creating your own list is an arduous and time-consuming task, but the result is invaluable. You may also purchase lists containing the information you need from specialist list companies and other sources such as some of the better résumé writing/career guidance companies.

The executives of the 500 or 1000 largest companies are bombarded with résumés. You might find it worthwhile to address your mailings to smaller, equally prestigious and growing companies.

The *Yellow Pages* is another good source of local company names, but does not provide names of executives and area codes.

In using lists and "broadcasting" your availability you take the best, quickest, and surest route to employment, other than knowing someone who can place you or having some other "inside track" to a position. Note the following in mailing your material:

- Address your letter or résumé to a specific individual by including the name on the envelope.
- If possible, include the individual's name on the letter as well, though this is not mandatory.
- If you are an upper-middle or top-level executive or administrator, send a sales or broadcast letter to one of the top executives or to the chief executive officer (by name).
- If you are a lower-middle executive earning, say $18,000 or less a year, send a covering letter and your résumé to the personnel director (by name, if possible).
- Make your initial mailing to 200 or 300 companies or more if possible, in order to obtain a satisfactory number of useful responses.
- Select as special targets for individualized letters those companies in which you are particularly interested.

103

Examples from *Advertising Age*

The following extract from *Advertising Age*, Section 2, "Job Hunting and recruitment," January 14, 1980, was written by the president and creative director of a well-known advertising agency:

One-third of agency recruitment sources consist of unsolicited letters and résumés. Here is a youngster sitting down to write one of the most important letters of his life, trying to break into a field where grabbing attention and selling one's merits are absolutely necessary. So how come aspiring admakers write such godawful dull letters? I've read hundreds, but only a few grabbed me by the tie and hoisted me out of my chair:

"Dear Mr. Jones: I think I have the makings of a really hot copywriter—in fact, you can see that this letter got singed . . ." She had burned the edges of the letter and envelope . . . She got her interview.

I remember a letter from a youngster who stapled a $10 bill to it, betting that he'd get an interview. I put the letter in a desk drawer and waited. Next week another $10 arrived with the message that it was now double or nothing. My guilt was such that I called him in and gave him back his $20. Also, I hired him.

"Dear Mr. Jones," writes a 26-year-old woman, "I've been everything from a truck driver to a Peace Corps technician, but I really want to write ads. I've had two years of college and read a lot. I'm working now in a boutique, and free lance for an East Side weekly. I think I know what makes people buy and I like selling . . ."

"Dear Mr. Jones: I'm a former *Playboy* bunny (38, 24, 36) and I'd like to make an appointment for an interview. . . ."

104

Do Something Different

The man who climbed one of the World Trade Building towers in lower Manhattan has become busy and well-to-do as a result of this stunt.

People who swim across the English Channel, to or from Cuba, or around Manhattan Island, sail around the world in a small boat, or try to cross the ocean in a balloon, expect and often get lucrative contracts or employment unrelated to the caper that first attracted attention.

105

A Job Safari

An unemployed job seeker could not find suitable employment in his home city. He decided to set out on a job safari, routing himself to major cities from Boston to Miami. He made no advance appointments. He did make a list of possible employers in advance, got referrals from friends, set out, and called selected executives in each city, asking for an interview. He said he was in town for only a few days and would like to discuss employment opportunities. Even if the person he called said there were no openings, our traveler said he didn't care, he would like to meet for a few moments and perhaps the company executive might have some ideas. He mentioned his qualifications and former business associations briefly, or a mutual friend if there was that connection. He was able to create many interviews and finally landed a job in South Carolina, an unexpected denouement.

People hate to turn down a candidate away from home who has enough motivation to travel away from it looking for a job. The inclination is to see him, particularly if he has reasonable credentials.

106

Install a Telephone Answering System

During the period that you are looking for a job, install some form of telephone answering service.

Many a position has been lost because an interested employer has been unable to get a candidate on the telephone. Repeated unsuccessful attempts become irksome. It doesn't happen often, but occasionally an employer is in a hurry to fill a position and will give interviews at once. If there are two or three people who seem to have the needed qualifications, the ones who can be reached quickly by telephone will get the interviews.

Any answer will commit the caller to do something—request a return call, seek the answer to a question, or make a date to meet—which is a tacit commitment to wait before hiring someone else.

107

Former Employer

Rehiring ex-employes used to be taboo at many concerns—but not any longer.

Most companies these days say they're more than happy to take back any former employe who was in good standing when he or she quit. "The days of discriminating against people who left previously are gone," says a senior vice president of New York's Chemical Bank. Heublein Inc.'s Kentucky Fried Chicken unit hires a former junior officer as its new president—even though he had worked in the interim for arch-rival Church's Fried Chicken.

The concept of corporate loyalty hasn't broken down entirely. State Street Bank & Trust Co., Boston, thought "long and hard" before rehiring a vice president who had quit twice previously. But generally, "We've kind of gotten away from the biting-your-nose-to-spite-your-face syndrome," says a bank executive. (*Wall Street Journal*, December 4, 1979.)

108

Have Your Résumé Circulated

Companies like Allied Stores, Associated Dry Goods, Associated Merchandising Corp., White Consolidated Industries, and many others have scores or hundreds of branches, divisions, or affiliates. By contacting one of them you may be directing yourself, for example, to every unit.

You may write to the headquarters office and ask that your résumé be circulated to appropriate affiliated companies. Offer to supply copies of your résumé. It will be better to provide your own copy lest your image be cheapened by poorly reproduced photocopies.

109

Secretarial Blessing

Some people have a knack for ingratiating themselves. If you can gain the approval of the boss's secretary, one way or another, he or she may be able to arrange an interview for you. If you possess this quality, you will be aware of many more ploys than the author.

110

Temporary Jobs

Employers often need temporary help during vacation periods, holidays (Christmas season, particularly for retailers), tax-due dates, advertising campaigns (art work), catalog preparation, and to meet unexpected emergencies.

A temporary job provides an easy path to an interview with your temporary employer for a permanent job. Many people who have signed up for temporary work have demonstrated qualities that lead to permanent positions.

Temporary jobs, too, may add valuable experience. They can effectively fill in what would otherwise be periods of unemployment in your résumé or employment application form. Accept temporary assignments while looking for full-time work.

111

Commentary: The Mature Executive

These are some general job-search directions for mature executives.

At the executive level, if you are over 45 years of age seek out small and medium-size companies and growth companies as employment targets. The reason is that giant companies promote from within; they prefer intracompany succession.

Exception: Some large conglomerated companies such as Beatrice Foods, White Consolidated Industries, and Alco-Standard are made up of many small semiautonomous companies with thin staffs and are therefore good targets for employment. (These are only examples, not specific recommendations.)

Large companies prefer to train their executives in their own methods; mature executives from outside are not welcome unless the company is a troubled one. Furthermore, pension and other benefits are costly to establish for older executives.

Note: This special training itself provides a reason for lack of enthusiasm for intercompany job exchange at mature levels.

Exception: Because women have only recently begun filtering into top-level jobs, their attainments may be recognized only when they are over 45. Highly qualified women are more welcome in the top corporate structure at age 45 and older than are men of the same age.

Caveat: If you are a specialist in a position that is typical only in a large company, you are most useful only in another large company.

For example: government liaison or lobbies; dealing with government regulatory agencies; patent licensing; E.D.P. systems development; environmental duties; utility rate studies; supervision of large clerical groups; product manager in a narrow or single-product line; check processing; petroleum marketing; and many more. Expand your responsibilities.

Salaries and benefits are frequently as high in small companies as in large ones, except at the very top levels of the giant companies.

Avoid taking a job with a company in a very small industry where there is no place to go if the company goes out of business, or you lose your job.

215

Exception: Positions in the financial area are industrially and commercially universal in character; the functions performed are common to all businesses.

Definitions: small company, up to $10 million annual sales; medium-size company, $10–50 million annual sales; growth company, one growing 20% or more a year.

III

Conduct Your Interview

INTERVIEW SECRETS

The First Big Interview "Secret"

Is there a secret to a successful interview? Yes, if you don't know the answer. Yes, if you do know it but don't use it. No, if you know it and exercise it. What is the secret? Preparation.
  What does preparation mean?

- You have practiced your part (role) to perfection.
- You know your qualifications (eligibilities, fittedness, or suit-abilities) and can speak with unhesitating authority about them.
- Your appearance is sufficiently neat and attractive that you are unconscious of it.

How long does it take to become prepared? Different lengths of time according to the individual: days, weeks, or months of practice, according to your capacity to absorb and live your role. Speed is not important. Perfection is.
  What words might help me understand this concept of preparation? Preparation is based on self-knowledge, ability to articulate, charm, poise, responsiveness, assurance, experience, integrity, enthusiasm, expressiveness, packaging, role playing, qualification.
  Some of these words are synonymous or overlap in meaning.
  Is preparation a guaranteed foolproof secret technique?
  No.
  Should I perfect my interview technique before having an important interview? Yes. Use less important interviews for practice.
  Can an unqualified person have a perfect interview technique? No, not with a knowing interviewer. Yes, with an inexperienced interviewer.

How do I know when my interview technique is perfect? When you can speak interestingly, unhesitatingly, and intelligently about yourself, or can look forward to an interview with pleasure rather than trepidation. If you enjoy interviews, you are ready to have interviews.

Suppose I have perfected my interview technique but continue to have unsuccessful interviews?

Review your "perfect" technique for flaws, or analyze your qualifications for deficiencies. Most people know, after an interview, what they did wrong.

Is it possible to have a perfect interview technique and still have unsuccessful interviews? Yes. Your "perfect" technique was not right for those interviews. Try again. It has been said, truthfully, that most interviewers don't pick the best candidates; outstanding candidates are often rejected.

The Second Big Interview "Secret"

The second big interview secret is: Recommendation. What does recommendation mean? It means that you have been approved for employment by someone whom your interviewer cannot deny. How can I make this work for me? By finding an individual of this kind who is willing to speak for you.

Obviously it would be helpful to be able to name a president, vice-president, cabinet member, member of the Supreme Court, governor, or mayor as a reference. There are also, however, powerful people in more limited circles who have equal or greater influence within those circles. These are "power brokers" little known to the general public.

Sometimes the mere mention of a name is sufficient to cause an interview to be granted.

There are two rules:

1 Be sure you are highly regarded by the person you name as a reference.
2 Be sure that the references you give are of sufficient importance to cause an immediate strongly favorable impression on the person receiving them. If you lack these two criteria, don't use references until asked for them, after a personal interview.

In approaching a prestigious law firm for employment some years ago the name of Chief Justice Charles Evans Hughes as a reference would have been persuasive.

In approaching IBM Corporation for employment, a recommendation by Thomas J. Watson would have been influential.

In seeking employment with any corporation the use of the name of a member of the Board of Directors as a reference would be effective.

The Third Big Interview "Secret"

The third big interview secret is: Accomplishment. What does accomplishment mean? It means that your record of past performance is so outstanding that it would be foolhardy for any company not to employ you. This "secret" may apply to only one in 10,000 people. How can I make this work for me? By expressing your accomplishments as strongly as possible.

The Fourth Big Interview "Secret"

What is the fourth big interview secret? Luck. What do you mean, luck? Luck is being in the right place at the right time with the special qualifications that meet a particular need. It is the chance convergence of favorable factors around you.

How can I make luck for me? Your chance of a lucky break will increase with the number of interviews you have.

The Fifth Big Interview "Secret"

What is the fifth big interview secret? Chemistry. What is chemistry? A compound of manner, appearance, and words that causes an interviewer to like you so well that he or she will lead you to the answers wanted, or will even accept poor answers to important questions and still select you for the position you are seeking.

How can I make this work for me? Create a "fragrance" constituted of charm, enthusiasm, and persuasiveness. Many have done it; you can do it, but it works only with some people.

Here are a few of the secret reasons for unsuccessful interviews. Your interviewer:

* Knows that the person you would be working for would not get along with you or you would not get along with him.
* Has been asked by an important executive to interview a certain person, but must make a show of interviewing others so that when the recommended individual is hired it cannot be said that undue influence was used.
* Knows that the opening is for a dead-end job and thinks you would not remain with the company after discovering it.

- Has a rigid salary limitation and must probably make do with a less-qualified candidate than he would like to hire, but nevertheless hopes he will make a lucky strike.
- Has been told he has to employ a person of a particular ethnicity or sex to correct E.E.O.C. problems in employee balance.
- Has been given an age limitation that he feels he must respect.
- Has a personal friend he wants to hire, but must go through the motions of interviewing others so that the reason for his selection can be camouflaged.
- Is faced with a last-minute change of mind about the kind of individual wanted.
- Experienced a breakdown in communications, so that he is recruiting for a different job than the one that is open.
- Does not recognize superior qualifications for unfathomable reasons: inexperience, insensitivity, indigestion, insularity, indiscriminateness, incapacity (cases of "in" meaning "out").
- Was away on the day of your interview and a less competent interviewer was substituted.
- Was up too late the night before or has a personal problem and is subpar in his reactions or interest.
- Is blameless. But you have misunderstood the nature of the position that is open and make an inconsistent presentation.

INTERVIEW RELATIONSHIPS

The interviewer/interviewee relationship is like a looking glass showing the reverse image of the same subject. The techniques are reversible. The advantage the trained interviewer has is that of a professional over an amateur.

As a good lawyer trying a highly technical case outside his area of expertise (medical malpractice, for example) becomes a temporary expert, so a job candidate should become a temporary expert in interviewing. The interviewer decides upon the question before he can elicit the answer. The interviewee seeks to know the answer before the question is asked.

When you are getting ready for a race, a heavyweight championship fight, a speaking appearance before an audience of 2500, a "Name That Tune" competition on TV, or singing "The Star-Spangled Banner" before a professional football game, you prepare, rehearse, and practice. I urge you to do the same prior to an interview. The ways to do so are many. Essentially they involve getting to know yourself and becoming comfortable with yourself.

Surveys make it clear that six to ten candidates are interviewed for every one hired. It makes no difference how the interview was initiated; most job candidates fail at the interview juncture of their job search.

If you know how to conduct an interview with a job applicant, you should know how to be interviewed. When you interviewed a candidate what did you want to know? A person who interviews you wants to know the same kinds of things; not only what your experience has been but also how you express yourself. The latter introduces your personality, the intangible factor upon which success or failure so often depends. It cannot be satisfactorily explained. There is a different chemistry among different people and the catalyst between one set of people is changed with another pairing.

In an interview you do not have to be a "yes" person. If you have strong opinions on subjects of importance, and are invited to do so, express them. A person without convictions is a nonentity. One need not be aggressive—and certainly a debate or a seeming invitation to argue is to be avoided—but ideas on inflation, employment, the stock market, takeovers, vacation spots, travel, well-known successes or failures and reasons for them, the FTC, interest rates, sports events, and government regulations are not necessarily to be avoided. Your thoughts about the important issues of the times may be more important to an interviewer than the nuts and bolts of your background. People in business are interested in business-related problems. People in nonprofit institutions are similarly interested in the business concepts that also affect their operations. It may, on occasion, be dangerous to express views outside the narrow context of a job interview; usually it is not, if you are a thinking person who can speak simply and economically. But don't ride a horse!

THE NATURE OF THE INTERVIEW

The interview between candidate and employer is for the purpose of exchanging personal impressions. It is usually weighted in favor of the employer and conducted in order to form a positive or negative decision with respect to employment. This is the arena of action—the moment of truth.

The larger the company the greater the potential number of barriers erected between the candidate and the employer in the form of interviews with various layers of management and perhaps the creation of data bases: credit reports, character investigation, psychological tests, handwriting tests, interviewer memorandums, résumés, recommendations (or the reverse) from former employers; each step adds to the complication of the decision-making, sometimes confusing matters more than clarifying them.

For who can *know* a person? An individual is the sum of what he shows and what he hides. Thoughts are a billion fireflies rampant in the mind, ranging from "shrieks and shapes and sights unholy" to the conventional, the banal, or to transcendental insights into beauty or innovation. The balance and control of thoughts are the factors that determine the man. Only the tip of the iceberg shows, except in the unbalanced person. A common question that people even ask themselves is "Who am I?"

You can approach an interview thoroughly prepared to sell yourself only to learn, after the fact, that you have been selling the wrong thing. Why? Because what the employer has said he wants may be different from what he really wants; and this can happen in a flash of understanding after a decision to hire has almost been made. Everyone who has been subjected to a number of interviews has had the experience of leaving an interview delighted with the rapport that seemed to develop, only to be left hanging in the air awaiting a decision for weeks, and finally learn that it is negative. From the interviewer's side this is no different from buying a house or a suit or a dress. You may enter the marketplace firmly determined on a new expanded ranch-style house only to fall in love with a center-hall colonial.

This book is concerned with the development of superior techniques in interviewing for a job at any level, from the interviewee side of the desk. There are other kinds of interviews: performance, counseling, career progress, and separation, which are primarily important to an interviewer; these are not addressed here.

Interviews change according to the level of the candidate:

Entry.
Middle management.
Top management.

and according to the level or interest of the interviewer:

Personnel assistant.
Personnel manager.
Vice-president, human resources.
The interested department manager.

The departmental vice-president.

The corporate president and/or chairman.

or according to the sex and race of the interviewer; or in accordance with how an outside agent such as employment agency or executive search firm is involved.

Caveat: Expertise in interviewing is no stubstitute for job effectiveness, as the following story illustrates:

Sam Lubbel had an interview with Vice-President Sussman of the Acme Apparel Company for a position as a salesman. He was so attractive in personality and presentation that Mr. Sussman was delighted. He had found an individual with experience, personality, and that indefinable thing called chemistry exactly suited to his needs! Sam was so good that it seemed important to hire him on the spot before he was grabbed by a competitor. Mr. Sussman had to clear Sam's employment with the president and took him into President Simm's office. After a brief conversation, Mr. Simm was equally impressed. They couldn't wait to put Sam on the payroll.

However, Mr. Simm's father, now about 80, came into the office for a few hours each day and his son, in politeness, decided to introduce Sam to old Mr. Simm. The elderly gentleman was busy with an old customer. Rather than have Sam wait around, they told him to come back later in the day, and expressed their pleasure in having met him. Sam departed, leaving some references.

The two officers congratulated themselves on their new employee. Just as a matter of form, Mr. Sussman decided to telephone the first reference on Sam's list, Mr. Graceman, whom Sussman knew slightly. Mr. Graceman said "Sam Lubbel? Yes, he worked for us. Confidentially, he's no good. We had to let him go after two months. My advice to you is don't hire him."

Mr. Sussman was a little taken aback by this response and decided to phone the second reference, a lady. Sam had characterized her during the interview as one of his best friends.

The lady answered Mr. Sussman's question. "Yes, I know Sam Lubbel. He's not a close friend, but I've known him socially for some time. However, I know nothing about his business qualifications and can't help you in that area."

The third person called was extremely evasive in his comments.

When Sam returned he was told the company had decided to defer a decision. Later Mr. Sussman discovered that everyone who talked with Sam for the first time was greatly impressed. But he could never keep a job.

The individual who recounted this tale went on to say how easy it is to be fooled by a person who has developed a superb interview technique; and how sometimes, in his experience, people who interview best turn out to be poor employees, while people who interview badly can become exceptionally good employees. Such embarrassing contretemps usually occur as a result of inexperienced or inadequate interview procedures.

COMMON DENOMINATORS

It is probably only happenstance that you are sitting on one side of a desk as an interviewee and another person is sitting on the other side as your interviewer. The situation might easily be reversed at some future time. Actually whenever one is employed, one is a potential interviewer.

Think of the things that the two may have in common:

Mortgage, debts.
The desire to earn money.
Family and friends.
The need to be liked and appreciated.
Success motivation.
A public face and a private face.
Education (possibly).

Some things that they do not or may not have in common:

The interview objective per se.
Politics.
Religion.
Social background.
Ethnic background.
Spending habits.

Look upon a job interview as a negotiation as in making a sale, drawing up a contract, or buying a car.

The job interview is like a sale. When you sell you provide a customer with a benefit. You explain the benefit. The customer compares it with others. Both buyer and seller enjoy a benefit when the sale is made. Many people are proud of their negotiating abilities, but don't think of

an interview in the same way. That's all it really is. (See example in
Chapter III under "Stress Interviews.")

Why does a company want to hire you?

1 To manage-administer-perform-function.
2 To back up-learn-grow-inherit (provide management continuity).
3 To make more money from:
   (a) sales
   (d) services
   (c) greater efficiency-productivity
   (d) expansion-merger/acquisition/disposal
   (e) invention-innovation
   (f) investment funds management
4 To save money through:
   (a) reorganization
   (b) production
   (c) purchasing
   (d) design
   (e) technology
   (f) union negotiations
   (g) turnover reduction
   (h) tax planning
   (i) insurance planning
   (j) systems
   (k) personal job objectives

Doesn't this immediately tell us something about the interview situation?

The goals on both sides are similar; on the one hand, to get the job;
on the other, to find a suitable employee. Subjects of mutual interest
are safe.

THE QUALITIES AN EMPLOYER LOOKS FOR

These are affirmative qualities. Under some circumstances, a few could be
negative. An interview is like unwrapping a mummy. What's underneath
all those bandages?

Personality Elements

Integrity.
Poise.
Ambition.
Compatibility.
Decisiveness.
Breadth.
Articulateness.
Enthusiasm.
Loyalty.
Sophistication.
Good taste.
Good health.

Work Effectiveness

Related experience.
Superior past performance.
Good education.
Favorable ideological attitude toward business.
Sound management style.
Technical mastery of discipline.
Equanimity under pressure.
Knowledge of industry.
Creativity.
Leadership ability.
Potential for growth.

An Employer Seeks to Identify These Negative Attributes:

Disruptiveness.
Poor past performance.
Pettiness.
Meanness.
Vindictiveness.

Laziness.

Dishonesty.

Lack of qualifications.

Ill health.

Alcoholism.

Neuroses.

Chronic credit problems.

Personality imbalances.

Poor family situation.

Inability to make a decision.

Some of the characteristics listed are self-evident (poise, articulateness) ; others require explanation.

Write down the definition of each word or phrase.

Write down for your own self-analysis and self-understanding how you would express the level of your excellence for each of the traits listed. (Yes, integrity can be expressed, as can ambition, compatibility, etc.) Write down, for the same reason, descriptions of your experience, your greatest accomplishments, any unusual aspects of your education. What is your management style—personal, group-oriented, organizationally rigid, or relaxed? Give examples of leadership, decisiveness, and other qualities. A picture of you begins to emerge.

Consider the negative qualities that employers seek to avoid. Do you have any of these attributes? If so, have you overcome them? It would be useful for you to write down how you have recognized negative characteristics in yourself and have overcome them.

What do you do with this material once it has been completed? Some of it you can use in résumé and/or letter preparation. The whole is an exercise in self-understanding that provides greater enlightenment when you write it down.

Writing disciplines thinking and eliminates the chance of fooling yourself as to exactly what you *really* know about yourself. Self-understanding is arming yourself in advance for an interview that formally or informally *must* result in answers to some or all of the questions implicit in the qualities named. *Regardless of the exact construction of particular questions, these are the essential employment-related facts to be learned about you or any interviewee.* Use this material to answer the question, "Tell me about yourself." Use it to answer your own question, "Who am I?"

*Hints for Finding Illuminating Answers to Some of the Less
Obvious Characteristics Cited:*

Integrity is ordinary honesty ("I don't steal"), as well as intellectual honesty. ("I am honest in my thinking as well as my actions.")

Decisiveness. Illustrate with an example within your businss experience. You decided to fire, hire, buy, make, alter, acquire, expand.

Breadth. What do you read? What great people in history do you most associate yourself with? What interests do you have aside from work and family?

Enthusiasm. Think of a situation in which enthusiasm has been an advantage for you (you were persuasive about a sale, an idea, a person). Samuel Goldwyn, a founder of Metro-Goldwyn-Mayer, said, "No person who is enthusiastic about his work has anything to fear from life."

Loyalty. Did you ever back up a business associate who had been unfairly maligned, even facing possible disadvantage?

Sophistication. Do you know how to order from a menu? how to dress to best advantage? how to introduce people? how to borrow money? Can you talk about new plays or books, new trends or ideas?

Good taste. Are you perceptive in knowing when certain words and actions are appropriate and when they are inappropriate?

Past performance. What have been your greatest achievements?

Ideological attitude toward business. Do you approve of the capitalistic system? Do you disapprove?

Creativity. Give examples of business activities that have been innovative with respect to your job.

Leadership ability. It could be illustrated with examples out of the past or in the present from your job or avocations, from community activities, from college days.

Potential for growth. Where did you start? Where are you now? What plans have you made to get where you want to go?

When you know what an interviewer is looking for and are prepared to provide answers to his search, you remove the cause for interview failure.

Get to know yourself. Put it in writing!

A good interviewer looks for characteristics according to the nature of the job.

Accountant	Professional preparation
Senior salesman	Aggressiveness, speech fluency, personality
Buyer (retail)	Knowledge of markets and prices, promotional know-how, acute awareness of trends

Financial executive	Technical financial knowledge
Marketing executive	Ability to plan, create, and lead
Production executive	Technical engineering background
Purchasing	Knowledge of markets and economics
Personnel	People-orientation, administrative ability

Most competent interviewers will try to put you at your ease immediately and then indicate that the interview is an exchange of information for the purpose of discovering mutual suitability. The environment presented is this: the job is open, the interviewer wants to fill it, let's see if we have a match.

One of the first questions will be why did you leave your last job or why do you want to leave your present position. Be prepared to express yourself fully. A good interviewer will use the silent treatment until you have. Don't gulp, hesitate, or be confused. Answer clearly and unhesitatingly. Some interviewers are highly intuitive; many managers are intuitive, able to draw upon past experience to provide solutions to curent problems. Perhaps the job requires that you, too, need to be intuitive. Your ability to do this may not be apparent from your recitation of your accomplishments. Your interviewer wants to know who you really are. Expect questions like, "In your business experience what things irk you?" "What do you consider your major accomplishments to have been in your last job?"

An intuitive interviewer will react to hesitations and incomplete or tangential answers. Such answers indicate your own doubt and where doubt exists in your mind, the interviewer wants to uncover the reason.

"Is your M.B.A. program completed? What was your M.B.A. course emphasis? Tell me what you did to achieve the accomplishments you have described."

Your reaction to unexpected questions, perhaps more related to an abstract idea than actual data on which you may be expected to be prepared, is observed and considered. Answers to such questions have nuances. The use of the word "we" or "I," for example, in describing accomplishments. A distinct change in the tempo of answers when confronted with abstractions rather than factual material. M.B.A. studies directed toward other objectives than the present job interest. Hesitancy about the date of any degree awards. Lack of knowledge of names of key accounts and their executives (if you are a salesman). Indirect answers to questions that can be answered directly. Physical reactions suggesting discomfort about a particular question. All unusual reactions are signaled in the mind of a skillful interviewer and call for further probing.

A simple question "What books have you read lately?" can throw some people into a tailspin; or "What historical personage do you most associate yourself with?" The questions have no relationship to your job abilities, but they test your reaction and response time to subjects remote from your immediate area of concentration.

Some interviewers use a technique, if they are interested in a candidate, of asking him or her to return at a later date with a list of questions that, if answered to the candidate's satisfaction, would enable him to make an immediate decision to accept the job (if it is offered). This enables the interviewer to determine the preoccupations of the candidate. Are they petty, related to security, or to fringe benefits? Are they more concerned with personal satisfactions than with challenges? Depending on the nature of the job, the questions asked by the candidate might be the determining factor in whether or not the job is offered.

An interviewer cannot learn anything about you unless you talk— so be prepared to talk to your advantage, alert to snares, booby traps, hidden holes, and uneven terrain.

What Interviewers Pounce On:

Evasions.

Hesitations.

Confusion.

Illogical statements.

Contradictory statements.

Unsupported claims.

Argumentativeness.

Weaknesses.

Ill temper.

Bad experiences in previous employment.

Before going to an interview, read at least the headlines in the morning paper to be aware of any recently developing important events that your interviewer might comment about. Try to form an opinion that you can express if the news is not politically, radically, or theologically sensitive.

FEAR AND OTHER CONSIDERATIONS

Fear at some level, slight as in uneasiness or stronger as in nervousness, is an emotion often present on both sides of the interview desk. On the interviewee's side, there are few situations that so undermine self-esteem as the feeling that one is not wanted or needed as when one is unemployed and in need of employment. On the interviewer's side, the fear is of making a mistake in selection. Hiring mistakes can be extremely costly. Hiring the wrong top executive, for example, could cost millions of dollars or even ruin a business.

The cost of a bad "hire" has been estimated by many personnel executives and other authorities and is seldom less than the lowest figures shown below. The figures are based on cost of training plus potential for damage:

Lower administrative levels	$ 4,000
Middle management	16,000 to $100,000
Top management	35,000 to $ millions

Because of fear, interviewers often compromise on candidates, choosing blander individuals lest those who show the most drive or other qualities might in the end be incompatible.

There are many aspects of a candidate that cannot be discovered in an interview. For example, that a candidate is finicky in small details; is unable to verbalize in daily business activities; is mean to subordinates; is subject to attacks of bad temper; is unable to admit mistakes; has an overactive sex drive; can't delegate authority; drinks too much; is egocentric; has a bad family environment; is disorganized, a poor administrator, or lacking in creative skills. All of these are hidden characteristics.

These are some of the reasons that interviews are not comfortable situations and can never be as easy as watching the Superbowl with a glass of beer handy. The interviewee is always a seller in a buyer's market, regardless of the organizational level of the interviewer. The interviewee is always in the position of having to satisfy the needs of the interviewer, which can range from initial information-gathering through assessment, referral to another with recommendations pro or con, to final decision after one or several meetings. The mere process of evaluation is humbling to one's self esteem; or perhaps more apposite, an interview is like taking an exam: "What questions will be asked that I don't know the answers to?" Whether in an interview or a classroom, the fear is of failure.

There are two words of supreme importance to a job candidate—"preparation" and "confidence"—and the first leads to the second. Barbara Walters says, "It is almost impossible to maintain poise when you are scared to death. My best advice for dealing with destructive anxiety is *homework* . . . homework helps enormously when you apply for a job." In order to be prepared, it is necessary to know what to be prepared for. Most interviewers have a checklist against which to measure qualifications, which would include job description, preferred experience, age, education, industry, personal attributes, plus perhaps psychological or other test results, your résumé, and other material.

If you were a recruiter you would have a prepared list of questions and a checklist to record general impressions. Expect that your interviewer will have this kind of preparation:

1 Get general impressions and write them down for future reference.
2 Be sensitive to poise, articulateness, and manner; pleasant, genial, tense, aggressive; responsive, easy.
3 Use company job description and candidate résumé to formulate a series of questions relating to specific qualifications for the job under discussion.
4 Ask of the interested managers what specific questions they would like to have answered.
5 Look for any negative signs such as neuroses, unusual reactions to sensitive questions, nervous disorders/illnesses, alcoholism (seek psychological testing if signaled).
6 Ask reasons for leaving previous jobs.
7 Ask for illustrations of most significant achievements.
8 Conduct a check on reputation and references.
9 Seek additional information about education and extracurricular activities.
10 (for an upper-level job) Create a profile of a manager and develop a series of questions that would halp identify such a manager. (Conversely, as a candidate you should know what constitutes a good manager and know how to answer questions directed to that end.)

Once competence is demonstrated, selection hinges on intangibles: character, compatibility, personality. Assuming one is qualified, or as qualified as any other, the intangibles take on great importance. There is chemistry between people; sometimes a catalyst exists, sometimes not.

Entry Level Candidates

Entry level candidates are of two kinds: those hired for clerical, plant, or other starting duties and not expected to be management material; and those hired for clerical or lower administrative functions and marked for possible management training. The first are usually hired through a personnel assistant; the second are first processed through a personnel assistant and then approved by the personnel manager. The second group is appraised for character qualities because inevitably, if they remain with the company long enough (and if the company remains in business), they will be successors to the present managers.

Middle Management Candidates

Middle management candidates are usually hired for what they know, their technical proficiency or special skills: computer technology, engineering disciplines, training procedures, advertising expertise, selling ability, research skills, writing, accounting, office management, and the like. Evidence of the education and skills sought is carefully investigated, first by a personnel executive, then by a specialist, then by a top departmental executive.

Top Management

Top management is usually cleared for further interviews by the top employment executive and then passed along to the interested top ex-

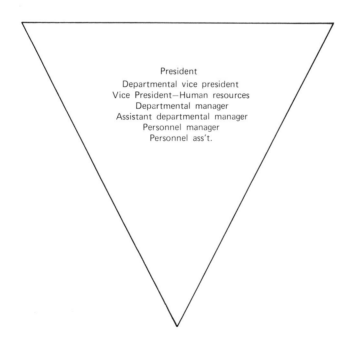

President
Departmental vice president
Vice President—Human resources
Departmental manager
Assistant departmental manager
Personnel manager
Personnel ass't.

ecutives at the company including the president and chairman of the board. Top management candidates are hired for more general skills than middle managers are called upon to express. The requirements are less tangible, with special attention given to such qualities as leadership, breadth, management style, reputation, decisiveness, assurance, as well as specific attributes like accomplishments, industry background, community involvement, health, social background and family life. Many top manager candidates once possessed the skills of middle managers but have moved along to creative and decision-making duties, which require the broader outlook that specialization tends to restrict.

The interview may be depicted as an inverted triangle, in which the nature of the give-and-take changes from narrower to broader questions as one moves up the triangle from lower level recruiter to president as recruiter. The interview could start or stop at any one of these levels, or move through several, according to the level of the position.

VARIOUS LEVELS OF INTERVIEWERS AND WHAT THEY LOOK FOR

The Personnel Assistant

The personnel assistant is usually assigned to hire lower-level employees and to screen other candidates. Such assistants may have special assignments: labor, clerical, or executive. In screening executive candidates he is utilized to get routine information but not to assess.

The Personnel Manager

The personnel manager is usually given hiring authority up to a certain salary level that may take him into the lower reaches of top management. He should be qualified to conduct interviews at any level and to make assessments and recommendations.

The Vice-President–Human Resources

This level is increasingly becoming a part of top management in recognition of the vital importance of selection to the health and progress of any organization. He can of course be overruled by anyone higher than he on the organization chart. He should be qualified to make judgments at any corporate level from chairman of the board on down—not individually, but as part of a team of top officers.

The Departmental Manager

The departmental manager is the best one to make a final decision about a candidate who will be subordinate to him unless his judgment as to people is in question, in which case the personnel manager will take precedence in making the final judgment.

The Departmental Vice-President

The departmental vice-president should have the final authority to hire anyone who will be subordinate to him and working closely with him (unless a change in management structure is contemplated).

The Corporate President or Chairman

These officers make the final hiring decision with respect to any candidates who will be working closely with them. They will base their judgments on the reports submitted to them and on personal and perhaps private criteria not used by any other interviewers.

The Employment Agency

The employment agency will assess candidates only in a general way to be sure that minimum requirements are met.

The Executive Search Firm

The search firm executive designated to screen candidates is in a very special position. He must be exhaustive in his investigation and evaluation of candidates. He must offer several candidates for the same job. He is also often called upon by the candidate for detailed information about the officers and the company that is going to interview him. For example, candidate Jones is aggressive and ambitious and reasonably happy with his present job. He is nevertheless interested in looking at any opportunities that might speed his career movement or give him special gratifications that he seeks: more money, more authority, more challenge, the chance to operate a company, the chance to build an empire. He wants to know from the executive search firm account executive:

- The nature and growth rate of the company, its P. & L. and balance sheet.

- Its share of market.
- The attitude of its top managers.
- The financial stakes of the top managers of the company.
- Family or other influences, if any.
- A rundown on the personalities, peculiarities, weaknesses, and strengths of the top officers.
- What power centers there are.
- Educational, family, and financial backgrounds of top officers as these might relate to their positions in the business.
- The ages, religion, ethnic background, and politics of the top officers—things he can't be asked by a prospective employer or ask of an employer.

After such exchanges of information the actual interview becomes only a ritual because each side knows just about all there is to know about the other and the only things left to exchange are banalities—or chemical reactions.

A word about chemical reaction. We all meet people to whom we take an instant like or dislike or who set up an emotional reaction in us after a few words of conversation. With experienced people it is sometimes very accurate. There is love at first sight. There is also intense initial dislike that turns into love. There is familiarity that becomes contempt; and there is the psychology of the love-hate relationship. Top-level interviews often turn on such intangibles, in complete disregard of pages of reports, analyses, and recommendations.

CHEMISTRY IN INTERVIEWING

The following is excerpted from an article that appeared in the September 19, 1979 issue of *The Wall Street Journal,* called "The Hidden Hurdle."

The personnel executive was as good as hired. During a *pro forma* final-stage interview, the board chairman observed that the job might involve a relocation later. "That sounds fine," said the candidate, "but of course I'd have to check with Mommy." "Mommy?" His wife. "Let's skip this guy," the board chairman said after the interview, to the executive recruiter. "If he calls his wife 'Mommy,' he might think I'm 'Daddy.' "

And that was good-bye to a $55,000-a-year-job—not the only one ever lost over a single word. Corporations like to say that competence overwhelmingly decides who gets managerial jobs. But executive recruiters say subjective chemistry—deciding whether the candidate is "our kind of person"—often is far more important than the executives doing the hiring realize.

The Big Factor "Chemistry is the paramount factor in hiring," says Wilhelmus B. Bryan III, executive vice-president of William H. Clark Associates, New York recruiters. Mr. Beaudine, who is president of Eastman & Beaudine, Chicago, adds, "More than half of the time, the technically best-qualified person isn't hired."

Decisive factors can range from significant questions of managerial style to finesse in eating an artichoke, recruiters say. In many cases, especially at the senior level, all the final candidates have such comparable proven track records that "chemistry becomes one of the major things to separate them," says T. G. Bartholdi, a recruiter based in Wellesley Hills, MA.

Chemistry counts more than ever these days, recruiters and executives say. Given today's operating styles and large staff bureaucracies, management involves more consultation and staff coordination than in years gone by, they note.

Seeking Risk Takers: Forced to evaluate this chemistry on the basis of a few interviews, employers latch on to all kinds of criteria that one might never expect, recruiters say. Burton L. Rozner, Executive Vice-President of Oliver & Rozner Associates, New York, recalls an entrepreneur who wanted an executive who personally was borrowed to the hilt. This entrepreneur, who operated a company with annual sales of $350 million, figured that heavy borrowers were just the risk-taking, self-confident, aggressive executives he had in mind.

One California engineering executive lost a job because he spoke with enthusiasm about coaching his son's Little League baseball team. In most cases, Little League might seem safe enough. But in this case, it "made the company president feel the executive's work wasn't really his top priority," says Robert Kremple, partner in Kremple & Meade, Los Angeles recruiters.

Physical appearance can cost jobs, too. Recruiters say trim executives often think chubby ones "lack self-discipline." John Wareham, president of Wareham Associates, New York, recalls an executive who was rejected as "too short" even though he was five feet, eight inches tall. "I feel you should look up to people in the finance industry," said the hiring executive—himself six feet, three inches tall.

Sifting Candidates. In the common situation where three or four candidates all could handle the job, executives often lean to people who share their personal values, manner of dressing, and even personal habits, recruiters say.

For instance, Mr. Rozner cites a $55,000-a-year pharmaceutical executive who landed a $90,000-a-year division presidency partly because he liked Victorian houses, hated television, and rarely allowed his children to watch TV, suggesting to the chairman a great similarity of values that would allow the two to work comfortably together, Mr. Rozner explains.

Recruiters say many executives sneer at candidates who wear short-sleeved shirts, short socks, or light-colored suits.

Artichokes were the Waterloo of one company president seeking the $300,000-a-year presidency of another consumer goods company. Though the executive was generally well polished, he revealed at dinner with the chairman a pitiable incompetence at handling the unfamiliar first course. At one point, he even tried carving the leaves with a knife and fork.

In most companies, senior management still is drawn from a remarkably narrow range of society, personnel officers note. In a survey of senior executives of the largest 750 companies, only eight of the 1708 respondents were women and only three were black. Some 95% were married, but only 11% had been married more than once. Nearly 70% were Republicans, and 92% identified with "conservative or moderate" views on social issues, said the study conducted by the University of California at Los Angeles and Korn/Ferry International, recruiters based in Los Angeles.

A Weakness. Recruiters say executives often don't recognize the chemistry that influences their hiring decision, especially when they're avoiding a strong executive who might prove threatening. "They often want an aggressive, dynamic person who is slightly less aggressive and dynamic than they are," says Mr. Wareham, the New York recruiter.

Many companies arrange for the prospective new hire and his wife to meet socially with other executives. A significant minority of companies also use psychological testing.

Given the increased attention to chemistry, the job that called for three interviews in the company five years ago often calls for five or six today, recruiters say. NCR Corporation, Dayton, also has prospects meet with more prospective peers than in the past.

"That's where the applicant will spend the majority of his time; jobs require more interaction than in the past," says William H. Von Reichbauer, director of corporate recruitment.

CHEMISTRY: INTERVIEW AT EXECUTIVE LEVEL

Richard Van B. Staley is founder and head of his health and beauty care company, looking toward retirement and seeking a replacement. He is talking with Claude De Bussey, who has been the successful president of the European branch of an American multinational company. Mr. De Bussey is a French national with a pronounced accent. He is magnificently dressed, with his hair curling long over his ears.

This is their hypothetical interview:

RS   Ah, my dear De Bussy, it is wonderful to see you. (There follows an exchange of amenities, recollections of past meetings, and congratulations by Staley on the excellent management performance of De Bussey.) Claude, I am going to retire. I intend to remain on the board. As a matter of fact, I will retain the title of chairman— but only until a satisfactory succession is completed. I have been thinking about you for the job.

CD   But I know nothing about your business—and I love Paris; it sings to me.

RS   I know your record very well, Claude. In place of specific experience you have management ability; and something else that I have and that the company needs—flair, style.

CD   Richard, you are too young to retire. You *are* the company. (Secretary knocks and enters.) "Mr. Staley, may I bring in some coffee?"
(Mr. Staley nods. The secretary is dressed in a strapless, fitted secretary/luncheon/dinner/dance dress. Mr. De Bussey's eyes follow her until she leaves.)

CD   Richard, she would be my secretary?

RS   You would have a staff of seven secretaries.

CD   No, no! I choose my own secretaries. I would choose this one. I I treat them all very well, *très bien?*

RS   Claude, I would be willing to pay you a $1 million bonus to come with this company.
(Secretary reenters, pours coffee after determining preferences, leaves with Mr. De Bussey's eyes following.)
Silence.

RS   Claude, did you hear what I said?

CD   Richard, I beg your pardon, I was thinking of something else. I feel terrible. I have a hangover.

RS   I said, 'I will pay you $1 million as an advance bonus if you will take the position I'm offering you.'
Mr. De Bussey stares out the window.

RS   I have operated this company for 40 years. I come in every morning at 8 o'clock.

CD   I am intolerable in the morning.

RS   I sometimes don't leave the office until 7 o'clock or later. I eat luncheon at my desk—just fruit or toast.

CD   Richard, I love your 21 Club and Morocco and Ciro's. Luncheon, for me, is a time of recharging. In Paris, my chauffeur drives me to the Bois—

RS   Claude, you can eat wherever you want. I'm just telling you what I do. My position is very demanding—and I'm getting tired and stale. That's why I want to pass the torch.

CD   Working 12 hours a day is stupid. As Hercule Poirot used to say, "The little brain cells—they are what count." In Paris, the girls, they are so beautiful, there is not time to work so long.

RS   Claude, are you married?

CD   Ah, yes. I have the lovely wife, chic, smart, diplomatic, the mother of my five children. Yes, we are a happy family.

RS   Claude, your income would be $350,000 a year in salary plus a bonus for performance that should be worth from $600,000 to $1 million a year. You would have a million-dollar insurance policy, a car with chauffeur, an apartment, a liberal pension plan, and a five-year contract.
(Secretary knocks, enters, removes coffee tray.)

CD   Richard, what is the name of your secretary?

RS   Claude, you are not listening to me. I want you to take over my job. I'll give up the chairmanship immediately. I won't stay on the board. Claude, we need someone like you here.

CD   Ah, Richard, you are so impulsive. In Paris we like to talk about things, to taste them, savor them, compare—to have a drink while we talk.
(It is 11:30 A.M. Mr. Staley pushes a button on his desk. The secretary enters. Mr. De Bussey appears to be lost in a contemplation of his own. Mr. Staley asks his secretary to open the concealed bar. Drinks are served. The secretary leaves. Mr. De Bussey seems to return to his surroundings.)

CD This is good, Richard. This is more like Paris. Now, what were you saying?

(Mr. Staley repeats his offer.)

CD Richard, you hardly know me. How can you be sure I am the man you want? I'm not sure I could live happily in New York. I do not sometimes understand your American idiom. Come to Paris with me. I will show you how to live. We will go to the Lido. I have a favorite entrée at the Ritz, which they do only for me and my friends. We will go to my pied-à-terre. I will introduce you—

RS Claude, just from being with you this brief time, I know you are the man we need. We must have you. I will give you $2 million up front. Do you know what that means?

CD Tax free, Richard?

RS (Long pause.) Yes.

CD I accept.

STRUCTURED, UNSTRUCTURED, STRESS, AND GROUP INTERVIEWS

Structured and Unstructured Interviews

Apart from standard interview procedures, you may meet two other types of interview situations in medium and large companies.

- The screening interview. The interviewer proceeds with a predetermined set of questions, with the purpose of determining your general suitability (i.e., fact-finding). Such an interview is usually conducted by a trained and experienced interviewer looking for holes in your background, but not specific job-related qualifications. This is called a directed or structured interview.

- The hiring interview. This will probably be conducted by the manager who will be your supervisor, and is not trained in interviewing. His interests relate to other responsibilities. The interview will follow a less patterned course. The interaction will move more spontaneously. This kind of interview is called undirected or nondirective, and the chemistry between two people is permitted to exert an influence. Also, in this interview your specific qualifications for the particular job will come into closer review.

Stress Interviews

You may meet still other situations. An interviewer might place you under stress by assuming an adversary attitude that is inquisitorial and demanding. Such an interview tests your poise. The questions that may be asked have to be within a reasonable perimeter, but they are asked with a different attitude. If you are prepared, the nature of such an interview should not bother you if you keep cool. If your interviewer is not relaxed, try to be relaxed anyway. If the tempo of questions increases, however, you should increase the tempo of your responses consistent with your ability to reply effectively.

One executive repeated this story to me about his early days on the road as a salesman. "In thinking about interview situations, I equate job interviews with sales calls. I recall many years ago visiting the buyer of a large department store. She had just agreed to give me the largest order I had ever taken, but had to have it approved by her merchandise manager. She took the order to her boss in a nearby office for his counter-signing. Instead of discussing the deal with her, he asked to talk to me directly. Here was an entirely different atmosphere. The merchandise manager was knowledgeable, quick, alert, adversarial, shooting questions at me like a lawyer cross-examining a witness."

Q Why will your line sell better than the one we have?

A It's the only nationally advertised line. We support our national advertising with cooperative advertising and with point-of-sale material to back up promotional advertising.

Q It's twice as expensive as the line we have. What makes you think our salespeople will sell it?

A We have a training program for salespeople. If you will permit it I'll conduct a training session, personally, anytime you say before your store opens.

Q Why are your products so high in price?

A Tests show that our products are better than most others—far better than those you carry now. Let me show you a comparison test. (Demonstrates.) People appreciate quality when it is explained to them.

Q Suppose they don't sell? Can we send them back?

A Over 200 of the largest department stores in the U.S. carry the line and have done so for more than five years. No one has ever had to send anything back because the line doesn't sell. But there are variations in neighborhood preferences by size and style. We have a standard policy of exchanging slow sellers for better sellers.

Q We need a 45% discount. Your line only shows 40%. Extend us a better discount.

A I can't give you a better discount. We'd be in violation of the Robinson-Patman Act—and we can't afford it anyway. The most important factor is I can produce sales of $400 per square foot and you have nothing in the department that will give you that big a return. You will make more money on our line at 40% than on other lines at 45%. In addition, you will have no markdowns, which now reduce your departmental gross profit by 4%.

"This merchandise manager (now the president of a major department store group) put me on my mettle to a degree I was not expecting, but I knew the product I was selling. It turned out to be a stimulating and enjoyable experience. The order was approved. I have enjoyed a continuing association with this man ever since our first meeting.

"Why do people who can express themselves well about their business become incoherent when they talk about themselves? The answer lies in these elements: lack of preparation, knowing yourself and your abilities less well than you know your business, built-in stress based on fear of failure. You fear you may not get another interview, whereas in business you think you can always find another customer to replace one you lost."

Interviews by a Group

Usually interviews are one on one. However, you may meet a situation where you are interviewed by two or more people, or by a board of directors. Try to keep in mind that several people come down to only one person—that is, you can respond to only one at a time. Handle this interview in that way. Talk to the person who asks the question. Try to avoid—do avoid—consciousness of self. Forget your physical self in the expression of your mental self—your answers to the questions.

In any interview restrain your enthusiasm if you become "sparked" by the response to one of your remarks. It may be a deliberate attempt to see how you react. At upper management levels calm and poise are highly valued.

PERCEPTION

The following was related to me by a close personal friend, currently a management consultant.

"I had a meeting with the president and vice-president of a corporation that over the last 10 years has acquired a number of smaller companies to create a broad-based tool group. The meeting was instigated by the president, whom I had known casually over a long period. I was intimately acquainted with a business they were thinking of acquiring and I had agreed to provide some data needed to help them make a decision.

"The president asked a series of questions of a rather routine nature. I ventured some additional information that I thought was important, but the meeting, which in my own mind I had scheduled for a full day, ran down by lunchtime. We all had lunch together and the president and his associate departed. I looked upon this meeting as a consulting assignment for which I would charge my standard fee. What I didn't know was that the decision to acquire had already been made.

"What I failed to perceive was that the president and his vice president were trying me out for size to determine if they should offer me the presidency of the new division. Had I looked upon the meeting in this light, I would have handled it entirely differently. Instead of data, I would have given them ideas about how the new division could be made more successful, of which I had many. I should have asked myself, "Are there other reasons for visiting me beyond the apparent ones? In other words I did not perceive!"

This kind of circumstance in infinite variety is true of many meetings. Sometimes a word, a remark, an attitude carry meaning beyond the seeming context of the conversation. Teach yourself to be aware of possible subtleties in any interpersonal conversation.

AWARENESS

A young lady applied for a job. The interviewer told her she was overqualified. She replied that she was anxious to have the position and would perform with pride and diligence. The interviewer was unreceptive. The young lady said she knew that the company was understaffed with women and quoted the Civil Rights Act of 1964 (Title VII), the Equal Pay Act of 1963, and Executive Order 11246. She got the job.

The Civil Rights Act of 1964 prohibits discrimination on the basis of race, color, sex, religion, or national origin. It is enforced by the Equal Employment Opportunity Commission.

The Equal Pay Act of 1963 applies only to sex discrimination in pay or benefits. It is enforced by the Wage and Hour Division of the U.S. Department of Labor, Employment Standards Administration.

By Executive Order 11246 federal contractors and subcontractors are prohibited from discriminating in employment because of race, color, religion, sex, or national origin. It is enforced by the Office of Federal Contract Compliance, which delegates its authority to contracting and administering agencies.

"NEVER, NEVER LAND" IN INTERVIEWING

List of nevers:

Never wear dark glasses.

Never wear a brown suit.

Never get too close to an interviewer.

Never wear flashy jewelry.

Never talk too much.

Never brag.

Never underestimate yourself.

Never be unprepared for any reasonable question.

Never make jokes, unless it is clear that your interviewer has a sense of humor and will react favorably.

Be neither overly formal nor overly friendly.

Never use first names on new acquaintance unless encouraged to do so.

Never smoke unless invited to do so.

Never shake hands like a "cold fish."

Never stare disconcertingly.

Never give the impression that you think you are better than the interviewer.

Never lose your temper.

Never say anything negative about yourself (having been fired is not necessarily negative).

Never smell of garlic or alcohol.

Never hide a disfigurement that cannot be corrected.

Never indicate that you are desperate for a job.

Never remain in the interview when your interviewer shows signs of wishing to terminate it.

Never criticize a former employer.

Never comb your hair during an interview.

Never let yourself be led into indiscreet personal comments or admissions.

Never appear at an interview with a hangover.

CONDUCTING THE INTERVIEW

Many books have been written about interview techniques. The subject is almost inexhaustible, involving philosophy, psychology, psychiatry, aptitude testing, common sense, and the variability of interview conditions. Here we present the basic considerations to make extensive further research unnecessary.

Who controls the interview? The answer is moot. Interview control is not an objective on either side. Rather, it is to exchange views between the interviewer who is the buyer and the interviewee who is the seller. The interviewer controls the interview when leading the conversation to desired topics. The interviewee controls the interview when discussing abilities and job qualifications with the greatest eloquence and knowledge.

In a sense you—the job applicant—are in control whenever you know what you are talking about and can express your knowledge properly. Hence our emphasis here on preparing for the interview. Before appearing for the interview consider how you will conduct yourself, the types of people you might meet, and the kinds of questions you might be asked.

Be certain that you can answer questions. You may think that you are knowledgeable in your area of competence only to find that an explanation requires specific data that you may have forgotten or an in-depth understanding of the subject that you lack, having thought about it only in a general way. For example, one seasoned executive talked about his career as ranging through staff and line jobs. When asked how he distinguished between them he floundered in his answer. The effectiveness of an interview is lowered when such situations occur.

In this section we discuss a wide variety of questions and give suggested answers to prepare you for your job interview. Whatever your answers to the interview questions given here, be sure that you have thought about them beforehand and are *prepared*.

"Catch" Questions

On the job your interests and those of your employer merge. During your job search, however, your interests and those of a prospective employer are in opposition until a mutual understanding has been reached. Asking unexpected "catch" questions is one method that a skilled interviewer will use to find out about you. Be prepared for them, and have your answers ready. Why did you leave your last position? Why do you want to leave your present position? What do you think you could contribute to this company?

Review the examples of interview questions given in the next section with your wife, sweetheart, brother, father, friend, or, best of all, a professional adviser.

Examples of Interview Questions

About Your Job Attitudes

1 What are your short-range objectives? Long-range objectives?
2 What do you look for in a job?
3 If we employed you, how long would you stay with us?
4 What new goals or objectives have you established recently?
5 What position do you expect to have in five years?
6 How would you describe personal success?
7 Do you not feel that you might be better off in a larger company? Smaller company? Different type of company? Different job classification?
8 Why do you want to work for this company?
9 If you had a choice, which job and company would you choose?

About Your Attitudes Toward the Position You Are Applying For

1 What interests you most about the position we have? The least?
2 What can you do for us that someone else could not do as well?
3 Why should we hire you?
4 How long would it take you to make a contribution to this company?

About Your Present or Previous Position

1 In your present position, what problems have you identified that had previously been overlooked?
2 What did you learn in your present position?
3 How would you evaluate your present company?

4 Why are you not earning more at your age?

5 Why do you want to leave your present position? Why did you leave your present position?

6 What do you think of your boss?

7 What features of your previous jobs have you disliked?

8 Describe a few situations in which your work was criticized.

About Your Social Attitudes

1 How do you feel about members of minority groups? Majority groups?

2 What is your attitude toward working for a woman? For a man?

About You

1 Can you work under pressure and deadlines?

2 What kind of salary do you think you are worth?

3 What is your biggest strength? Weakness?

4 If you could start over again in your career, what would you do differently?

5 Will you be out to take your boss's job?

6 How would you describe your personality?

7 What do your subordinates think of you?

8 What makes you believe you have top management potential?

9 Tell us all about yourself.

10 What was the last book you read? Movie you saw? Sporting event attended?

About Your Management Philosophy and Job Approach

1 What is your philosophy of management?

2 Do you prefer staff or line work? Why?

3 How have you changed the nature of your job?

4 Have you ever fired anyone? Why?

5 Have you hired people before? What do you look for when hiring someone?

About Your Accomplishments

1 Are you creative? Illustrate.
2 Are you analytical? Illustrate.
3 Are you a good manager? Illustrate.
4 Are you a good leader? Illustrate.
5 Have you helped increase sales? Profits? How?
6 Have you helped reduce costs? How?
7 What are your five biggest accomplishments in your present or last job? Your career so far?
8 Did your company make money under your management?

Offbeat Questions

1 Why have you been out of work so long?
2 What other positions are you considering? What companies?
3 Are you interested in causes? If so, what kinds?
4 What do you think of the business outlook over the next year or two?
5 What do you think of the present investment climate for an individual investor?
6 Do you think that busing schoolchildren is good or bad?
7 Do you believe in capital punishment?
8 Do you think that parents generally are too permissive (not permissive enough) in raising their children?
9 Do you think, from your experience, that labor unions were good or bad for (a previous employer)?
10 Do you think that welfare expenditures are too high (too low)?
11 Which senator (or congressman) do you most admire and why?
12 Would you be willing to work for a homosexual?
13 Do you plan to be married?
14 What activities, outside of your work, do you engage in?

THE 20 MOST EMBARRASSING QUESTIONS

I was once asked to list the 20 most embarrassing questions for a job candidate to answer. This seemed straightforward enough until I thought about it. The embarrassing questions are the ones that any given individual has difficulty in answering.

I know one man who was embarrassed for years when anyone asked him where he went to college. He had attended evening classes at a state college, but all his friends had gone away to prestigious universities. He recovered eventually, but for a while he stammered about it.

Another person was upset when asked about recent reading. Actually she read about four books a week, often without being able to recall authors or titles.

One man, asked in an interview to name a famous person in history with whom he most closely associated himself, stumbled around for an answer even though "Teddy" Roosevelt had been his hero since the age of 10. An intelligent answer would be that such associations changed with the various periods of your life.

It is unexpected questions that sometimes cause the most trouble. No question is embarrassing if you are prepared for it.

In my opinion, in general, the 20 most embarrassing questions would be:

1   Why did you get fired?

2   Why haven't you been more successful?

3   Why is your salary so low?

4   Why didn't you finish school?

5   Why do you want to work for this company?

6   Tell me about yourself.

7   Why do you want to leave your present position? (or Why did you leave your last position?)

8   What are your greatest weaknesses?

9   Tell me about your most important achievements?

10   What is your current salary?

11   What do your associates think of you?

12   Describe your job growth.

13   Why have you made so many job changes?

14   What mistakes did you make in your last job?

15   How do you get along with your boss?

16   What do you do in your spare time?

17   Why were your grades so low?

18 What do you look for in a job, security or challenge?

19 Why can't we get any favorable references?

20 What features of your previous jobs have you disliked?

STYLES OF MANAGERS

"What is your management style?"

Describe your management style. If you do not have a readily identifiable style the following answer would be acceptable to many people:

"I prefer a loose organizational structure to one that is rigid. I test and train my managers thoroughly. When I know that they can be depended upon, I like to delegate authority to them. I form corporate objectives and use them as my own guide. I like to develop strategies, discuss them, test them, and then act on them. I use data to make discoveries.

"Where decision-making is judgmental rather than factually oriented I use my judgment, as for example in product design. I have been very successful in utilizing this method.

"I dislike frequent meetings—too often they are unproductive, but I am receptive to advice and counsel.

. "I believe that decisiveness is necessary and think that sometimes indecisiveness is worse than a wrong decision. In general I have made the right decisions most of the time."

These are management attributes reflecting the psyches of individual managers:

Compromising	Uncompromising
Benevolent	Tyrannical
Decides by committee	Decides individually
Takes no risks	Takes chances
Works hard personally	Delegates
Recognizes merit	Overdemanding
Empathetic	Disregards feelings of others
Exercises relaxed leadership	Drives
Prefers loose organization	Tight, structured organization
Business stability	Business growth
Autonomy of divisions	Central control

It is easy to describe methods by listing a positive trait and then entering its opposite. However, these traits are not intended to be descriptive of a kind of manager. The methods used to operate can be intermixed or changed under different conditions. The same manager can be both compromising and uncompromising or both tyrannical and benevolent depending on people and situations. A good manager is flexible. Seemingly, opposite characteristics often balance each other.

There are other differences among managers growing out of training and personal inclination. Some individuals are people oriented, others are production oriented. Managers who handle people well have these qualities:

Leadership
Potential.
Integrity.
Empathy.
Charisma.

Managers who are aggressive in their drive for the productivity of their employees have these characteristics:

Knowledge.
Motivation.
Decisiveness.
Profit orientation.
Creativity.

A recent book entitled *The Gamesman* by Michael Maccoby (Simon & Schuster, 1977) puts managers in four general psychological types with these characterizations:

1 The Jungle Fighter. Overriding with respect to others, autocratic, dedicated to objectives, demanding, motivated by money and power, competitive. Weaknesses: may take strong course in wrong direction; antagonizes others.

2 The Craftsmen. Experts in various fields: scientists, engineers, marketers, financial managers, problem solvers. Competitive with respect to ideas instead of people. Possess personal pride in their own areas of expertise rather than in trying to reach the top spot. Weakness: possibly lacking in breadth for top-management responsibilities (but this is not necessarily so).

3 The Company Man. Dedicated to the company as it is. Combines personal and company goals. Subordinates self to company. Rises slowly through the ranks. Comprehensively experienced in all facets of job, whether at the top or lower. Weakness: slowness to recognize necessity for new approaches.

4 The Gamesman. Wants to change from the status quo for his company and to lead the change. Willing to take calculated risks to gain recognition and enjoys the sport of winning the competitive race. Uses team approach. Often magnetic, with strong leadership qualities. Innovates, develops others, delegates responsibility. Weakness: vision may be flawed.

Managers are not all of one kind or another. Qualities overlap, of course.

When weaknesses in managers do show up they do so in unexpected ways: writeoffs of company failures (Westinghouse, Singer, RCA, in the past); slowness to recognize improvement in technology (Gillette, the steel companies, the tire companies); failure to recognize trends (the "Big Three" auto manufacturers); integrity overcome by ambition (many companies); intolerance of the ideas of others leading to leadership failures (Singer in the past). The list could be expanded to include hundreds of other companies. Weaknesses often do not show up quickly, or if they do, they may be overlooked by reason of the system of modern management that gives tremendous authority to its chief executives; fortunately the system is more often right than wrong, and of course management can be wrong but profitable.

Companies seek executives who have no weaknesses. It is a fruitless search. Good managers grow as their responsibilities increase and they overcome their weaknesses. Others are flawed from the start, but with the cracks appearing only when the human engine is worked at top speed over a long, rough course.

The personality danger signs are: indecisiveness, instability, irritability, stubborn pursuit of the wrong goals, pettiness, meanness to subordinates, cronyism.

Frequently the chief executive officer has been selected because he can bring to a company special qualities: vision, drive, motivation, enthusiasm, leadership, and the rest; or he may have been selected for other qualities: experience, prudence, knowledge, or maturity, which are psychologically different from the others mentioned.

Some executives approach their new jobs diffidently and humbly, but grow to a perfect fit; others come into them like a strong wind, confidently, and assured that whatever they do is right.

INTERVIEW QUALMS

People's problems with questions are usually the result of an insufficiency, or the fear of an inadequacy.

We have all known typists who claim a certain kind of experience, a level of speed or accuracy that is immediately discovered as misrepresentation by tests. However, even superior typists are sometimes so nervous under the eye of a possible new boss that all their skills desert them. So it is with many people. Lack of confidence in themselves destroys their ability to show their true competence.

Sometimes what one thinks of as deficiencies are only seeming deficiencies. The more one knows of people and how they handle their jobs—their doubts, fears, fancies, indecisions, ignorance, inexperience of many aspects of a problem—the more one realizes that most people have the same qualms as the job candidate who is nervous in his interview.

The other side of the coin is that people do apply for positions for which they are unqualified and hope the questioner will not discover it. Embarrassing questions are when the drill hits the nerve. Nonetheless, some people claim to love interviews.

CHARACTER QUESTIONS AND KNOWLEDGE QUESTIONS

It may be too obvious to mention that if your career is in a knowledge area—engineering, science, teaching, law, medicine—you can expect interview questions directed to your specialty, in addition to the questions about your character.

Management science, for example, is a part of the whole of management. The practice of management science demands the mastery of techniques. One does not need to be a management scientist to be an excellent manager, but an excellent manager will use the management scientist specialists to help form opinions and make decisions in the same way that he or she uses lawyers, engineers, researchers, chemists, physicists, or any other support functions. In these specialties you need to know facts, procedures, and methods. In such interviews the interviewer must be a specialist to recognize the quality of the interviewee's qualifications.

Only a trained specialist can utilize regression analysis, variance and covariance calculations, null and alternative hypotheses, probability statistics, nonparametric techniques, and the like.

One's knowledge of heat treating, metallurgy, die-making, forging, stamping, extruding, and electromechanics can be measured only by another person trained in these disciplines.

Similarly, to direct a successful advertising agency, one does not have to know production techniques, but a production manager must know about mechanicals, printing, typography, and many more technical operations to be effective.

In the interview the specialist must know a great deal about a limited area; the generalist must know a little bit about every area.

EXPRESSING YOURSELF

If your field has developed a jargon that is well understood and commonly used in your vocation or profession, express yourself in that special language to those who know but avoid it at higher and lower levels if it might not be understood. This is particularly true in certain advertising and computer-related positions and with respect to certain disciplines (public relations, show business, art, economics, for example). Try to find out in advance what kind of person you are having an interview with, a generalist (such as a recruiting executive) or a specialist (such as a department manager or supervisor), and conduct yourself accordingly.

USEFUL INTERVIEW PROPS

Props give direction to interviews, help overcome nervousness, and provide supporting evidence.

Photographs.
Proofs.
Tear sheets.
Samples of crafts.
Letters of recommendation.
Scrapbook of articles or mentions.
Packaging.
Books, speeches, theses, dissertations.
Architectural drawings.
Résumés.
Graphs.

Presentations.

Awards, honors.

List of references.

Family snapshots.

It may be comforting to have them—but unnecessary to use them.

SUGGESTED ANSWERS TO INTERVIEW QUESTIONS

The most common interview question is: "Why did you leave your last job?" or "Why are you thinking of leaving your job?" Be prepared with *your* answer and be honest. Many answers will be self-explanatory. Your company might have been acquired by another company, in which case the employees of the dominant company will be given preference. Loss of business or profits requires layoffs. A new manager, brought into a company from outside, might want a new staff or might bring his own staff. Perhaps you were bored and your work showed it. There are also personality conflicts, internal politics, power plays, family incompatibilities, and nonconformance to a corporate pattern. *Basically, any separation is due to someone else's being preferred for your position.* Even a separation caused by loss of business indicates that you, in your job, could not influence the loss in a manner favorable enough to justify your retention. In a viable company some people will always remain.

A personality conflict is a common reason for a job change and is affirmative for you. You recognized a situation and made a decision (or it was made for you). Most people realize that one man's meat can be another man's poison.

In being honest about your reason for leaving a company, you can nevertheless discuss it in as favorable a manner as possible, often turning it to your advantage. If you *were* bored, for example, say that your position lacked challenge.

Be judicious in talking about a former employer. Do not indulge your inclination to castigate the employer, even if it is deserved, since such a negative attitude will serve as a red flag signal to an alert interviewer: "If this is the way the applicant feels about a former employer, how is he or she going to feel about us?" Instead, speak in general terms about the fact that some people simply do not get along well together and that therefore you are in search of a more compatible situation. Do not allow a negative attitude to destroy an interview.

If you were fired, you can either (1) admit it and explain why or (2) not admit it, say you resigned, and explain why. Most former employers speak about their former employees euphemistically. Firing an employee can be an employer failure, too.

Suppose you were a salesman with a territory. Your territory lost sales, instead of gaining them. You were fired. There could be these reasons for your failure: the salesman who preceded you ruined the image of the company; the company would not make the policy changes you recommended and you became discouraged; essentially you did not like the products you were selling or the kinds of customer you had to call on. Or the company did not reimburse you adequately for your expenses. And so on.

Or you were an office manager who was very hard to get along with. Your subordinates complained, and you were fired. Admit your former deficiencies and claim to have overcome them (and make an effort to do so).

You were a research director for a large company; you were fired. If you were really qualified for the position, there must be a very good reason (favorable to you) why you failed. If you were not qualified, you must be honest with yourself and search for a position at a slightly lower level for which you are qualified.

You were a plant manager. You could not attain the production increases required. You were fired. The various processes are sufficiently complicated to be able to find a hundred reasons for the termination that are not your fault.

You were an automobile salesman. You sold very few cars. You were fired. You discovered subsequently from a salesman with whom you had worked how to sell cars when he sold you one. It was one of the great lessons of your life from which you have profited.

You were an alcoholic. You did not carry out your business responsibilities. You were fired. Subsequently, someone in whom you had great confidence helped you. You have recovered from your problem and are now capable of meeting your responsibilities. Explain it.

You had a boss you liked. His boss did not like you. You were forced out of the company. Explain what happened.

You were an advertising manager. You made plans for a promotional campaign involving a lot of paper. The plan was approved and suddenly canceled. You were committed to your printer for special paper and the company was forced to pay for it. You were fired. It should have been a good lesson. Admit it.

You were operating under a budget. Suddenly expenses that you had not foreseen put you well over budget. Important plans had to be curtailed. You were fired. It is hoped that you benefited from the experience. Explain it.

You are a stenographer. Your work is slow and inaccurate. You were fired. Correct your deficiencies, or expect to be fired over and over again.

The question, "Do you prefer staff or line work?" is an interesting one. Make sure you know the difference between line and staff responsibilities. A staff position is one that supports a manager who executes; it is advisory. When a function becomes important enough, a manager will assign an aide to supervise that function. Examples of staff jobs are director of research and development who reports to someone other than the chief executive officer; product manager; corporate attorney; marketing research director, E.D.P. manager; planning director; or any assistant. A line position is one requiring execution rather than advice. The top manager of any function who makes a decision that is carried into effect is a line manager with respect to that function, but may be staff in his relationship to his superior. Examples of line positions are chief executive officer; vice-president of marketing; vice-president of finance; vice-president of production; salesman; regional manager; divisional manager; sales manager; department manager.

In rising through the corporate ranks, one will hold both staff and line positions. The answer to the question posed is that you prefer any position, line or staff, where you learn more about the company and can contribute effectively and measurably to some facet of management. Ultimately you want line responsibility.

"What are your long-term objectives?" A reasonable answer would be: to develop your own capabilities and learn enough about the operation of the vocation in which you are engaged to make a maximum contribution (to profitability) (to more efficient operation) (to better executive development planning) (to corporate growth) (to better administration) (to improve education) (to gain knowledge) and to continue your development and learning throughout your career, in order to achieve the life-style most consistent with the desires and hopes of your family and yourself at whatever your job level may be.

A short-term objective is to take the earlier steps necessary to accomplish the long-term objective.

"What position do you expect to have in five years?" Whatever your job level, you expect to have a *better* position in five years. You will have a better position if you are promoted or if you bring new ideas and achievements to the same position. You also expect to have a position that is consistent with your ability to contribute to the aims of the organization for which you work; and *you expect to have a continuing learning opportunity.*

If you are not ambitious, you may be happy with the routine of a familiar daily role. There is nothing wrong with this if you understand that the key word is "happy"; however, do not express this point of view to a prospective employer.

Below are a number of possible interview questions and suggested answers to them.

1 "What do you look for in a job?" Personal fulfillment consistent with effective administration.

2 "If we employed you, how long would you stay with us?" As long as you permitted me to learn and advance at a pace consistent with honest objective and subjective appraisals of my ability.

3 "What new goals or objectives have you established recently?" If young, you may have just decided on the career you want. If older, you may have learned that you have gerater talents in one area than in another and have now decided to concentrate in this new area. Or your objectives may have been established some time ago and you are still pursuing them.

4 "How would you describe personal success?" Complete fulfillment of one's capacities to develop and contribute.

5 "Don't you feel you might be better off in a (larger) (smaller) (different) type of company or in a different job classification?" If you did have a specific reason for choosing that particular company, explain it. It is a silly question, but do not show that you think so. Ask the interviewer to answer the same question. You might learn something.

6 "Why do you want to work for this company?" This is the kind of question the answer to which would vary greatly according to the kind of position you are looking for. For example, you might want to work for the company just because you need a job and would be willing to work for any company. Or you might want to work for it because you have special expertise that would be particularly effective if put to use. You cannot, of course, give the first reason. Say that you want to work for the company because of reputation, location, growth, substance, opportunity. If seeking an upper-level job, you should know the answer from your research.

7 "If you had your choice among companies, what company would you most like to work for?" To answer this question intelligently

would require an almost encyclopedic knowledge of corporations and institutions. The best answer is probably, "A company like yours," which leads then to the answers given to the preceding question.

8 "In your persent position, what problems have you identified that had previously been overlooked?" You will find your answers to this question by a reference to your résumé in which you have expressed your accomplishments.

9 "What interests you most about the position we have available?" It coincides with your abilities and interests. "What interests you least?" is an inappropriate question to which you could not give any other answer than that you are unaware of uninteresting aspects. A better question would be, "What aspects of the position are least attractive to you?" The answer could be too much travel or too many administrative details, but they are aspects that you are willing to accept as a learning prelude to a better position.

10 "What can you do for us that someone else could not do as well?" Relate your past accomplishments.

11 "Why should we hire you?" Same answer as above. "How long would it take you to make contributions to this company?" How old is Ann? You learn quickly; you are experienced; you are professional; you reorganized a section, a department, a business in such and such a length of time. You work as hard as necessary to acquire the particular skills as quickly as possible.

12 "What did you learn in your present (or most recent) position?" This is a good question because your acceptance of continuous learning is a primary element in an evaluation of you. You should learn from every job. When you stop, look for another position. If you did *not* learn anything in your present or recent job, go back to any situation where you did learn something. You may also explain that failure to learn in a recent position is one reason you are seeking new employment. This should not be a difficult question to answer.

13 "How would you evaluate your present company?" An excellent company *but* (with respect to you) too small, too large, too structured, too slow in growth, not enough new products, .offers limited opportunity, losing business to competition, no employee benefits, poor salary structure, and so on. This should be an easy question to answer. Do not divulge confidential information to a competitive company at this stage of negotiation.

14 "Why aren't you earning more at your age?" Opportunity was more important than money. You have learned, but the oppor-

tunity you sought has not developed as you expected. This is a major reason for wanting to make a change. If you are seeking an income well above your present earnings, be ready to explain why you are worth more. For example: "I have been exposed to a wonderful learning opportunity during the last year (last few years) and I have taken advantage of it to the point where I am now able to handle expanded responsibilities."

"I have learned how to exercise the responsibilities of the job levels above my present position and am looking for a position that will provide me with much larger responsibilities. The opportunity is not available in my company at present."

"The company I work for has been suffering from lack of profitability and salary levels have been frozen for the last two years."

"My company provides great security, excellent fringe benefits, and extra holidays that formerly satisfied but no longer do. I prefer opportunity and challenge to security."

"I remained with the company until I completed my M.B.A. program, which has provided me with insights that now make me more valuable."

15 "What do you think of your boss?" Even if he is an s.o.b., do not say so. You respect and admire him for his good qualities. If you do admire him, tell why.

16 "What features of your previous jobs have you disliked?" Do not answer this question too hastily. Answer in general rather than in specific terms.

17 "Describe a few situations in which your work was criticized." For example:

It was within my responsibilities, as written in my job description, to establish company terms of sale. I extended our terms from a dating of 30 days to one of 60 days to meet competition and increase business. The (new) president of the company criticized me for making the decision without consulting him, even though I had been making the same kinds of decisions for many years.

I developed a new and needed product. I was criticized because the new product made some other products obsolete.

I took a job in a factory involving the disassembly of old fire extinguishers. The foreman criticized me for working beyond the normal speed of the production line.

Always try to give examples of criticisms that put you in the best possible light.

18 "How do you feel about people from minority groups?" You are neutral. You would work for or employ any person who is qualified. You would not want to work for anyone less qualified than yourself. Nevertheless, the situation of a less-qualified individual supervising one who is more qualified is common. You may be in such a situation and now trying to extricate yourself from it.

19 "What is your attitude toward working for a woman (or a man)?" Again, you are neutral and would work for or employ any person who is qualified. You should, however, be fully aware of any bias you might have, so as to be able to correct or handle it with as little detriment to your career planning as possible.

20 "Can you work under pressure?" This is not a good question. People respond to crises in very different ways, handling one crisis with difficulty and another crisis with assurance. Basically one works under pressure according to one's training to meet a particular kind of situation, such as delivering merchandise to a customer or delivering a baby—a crisis or a routine, depending on one's training. The answer to this question is yes if the crisis is within one's general competence and experience. The experienced individual who does not know how to handle a situation admits it and seeks time to find a solution.

21 "What kind of salary do you think you are worth?" If qualified for the position, you are probably worth more than the employer is willing to pay. This does not mean that you would not be willing to accept the level of pay offered. The question is without real merit, but gives you a chance to value yourself. A capable executive generates more than 40 times his cost in profits.

22 "What is your biggest strength?" The question is susceptible to a million answers. The ability to see what needs to be done and to do it personally or by delegation. Leadership. Knowledge of the industry. Knowledge of the markets. Knowledge of whatever is the specialty under consideration.

23 "What is your biggest weakness?" Turn this question to your advantage. You are impatient. You want to see a job done quickly and expeditiously and sometimes are critical if you think the work is progressing too slowly. You are apt to say what you think instead of being a yes man. This sometimes gets you into trouble with a superior who is intolerant of disagreement. You are stubborn. If you know you are right you maintain your position despite the possibility that by giving up your viewpoint you would make yourself better liked by others. Some will see such

traits as weaknesses (lack of diplomacy), but enlightened employers usually like them. In politics one has to compromise, but compromise can be the death of business.

Someone has said "What is your greatest weakness?" with respect to getting a job, "You are screened in because of your strengths, and screened out because of your weaknesses."

In the old West you would never have admitted that you were a horse thief, or a cattle rustler, or a squatter on a railroad right-of-way.

Modern work weaknesses are indecisiveness, ill temper, bad health, pettiness, underqualification, and so on. Overriding all other qualities is the ability to get the job done; if you can do that, you have no important weaknesses. Don't admit any except unimportant weaknesses. If you have learned never to make the same mistake twice, you will not have any important work weaknesses. Interview probing of this kind is a shot in the dark of little value to an interviewer unless you are stupid enough to express an important weakness. If you are petty, you'd better get over it. If you are indecisive in your job, you're probably not qualified for the job you're seeking.

A good "weakness" would be taking extra time to help others overcome their problems, rather than summary discharge for a single mistake. Another good "weakness" is acknowledgment that you don't know everything. Everyone has weaknesses. If one is aware, the weaknesses should disappear. If they don't, one has a *real* problem. You can always talk about weaknesses you once *had* and that you have overcome. That's the real answer to the question.

24 "If you could start your career over again, what would you do differently?" Perhaps you would not have remained so long with your last, or previous, employer. Possibly you would have been stronger in pressing your point of view. Maybe you would have sought outside advice for a situation that needed an objective approach.

25 "Will you be out to take your boss' job?" In general, yes—with the hope that your boss will also be qualified to move up.

26 "How would you describe your personality?" In general, your personality is one that develops affirmatively in your dealings with other people, as they come to know you better.

27 "What do subordinates (associates) think of you?" They either like or dislike you, but always respect you.

28 "What makes you believe that you have top management potential?" Because you have superior insight and foresight; the ability to motivate and delegate; the capacity to get things done; the skill to choose the right people to accomplish the jobs that need doing and to inspire their loyalty; the talent to be right more often than wrong; the willingness to do yourself what you would ask anyone else to do; integrity, reliability, dedication.

29 "Tell us all about yourself." You should have prepared yourself by following our earlier advice to learn the elements of your résumé by heart.

"Tell me about yourself."

This is the invitation you have been seeking. It has thrown some job applicants. It will never be a hurdle to you if you are prepared. The job you are seeking is vice-president, marketing. Example of reply:

"I have had a successful career in marketing. I have led a sales force to extraordinary accomplishment, to the point where our organization is the envy of the industry. I have reoriented our sales strategy so that our share of market has risen from 25% to over 50%. I have supervised R&D in the redesign of some of our lagging products to make them best sellers. I have increased our sales over 10 times in the past five years, and with this expansion have positioned my company financially to make production improvements adding to the efficiency of our products and lowering our cost, adding 6% to our profits. I am recognized throughout my industry as its most progressive executive. I can accomplish the same kind of results for your company."

"Let me tell you a little about myself.

"I am the managing editor of a national magazine, with circulation in the millions, third in the hierarchy of management.

"I was recruited for this position three years ago and during my tenure I have improved the layout and appearance of the pages, installed automated printing at a great reduction in cost, balanced editorial material and advertising to provide a better mix, and improved profitability by just over 30%.

"During my career I have been the editor of several newspapers with a consistent and uninterrupted record of increasing circulation and gaining dominant share of market.

"I started as a reporter and worked for the *Herald Times* for two years in order to uncover the background of the 'French Connection,' leading to the arrest and conviction of a gang of 250 international drug gangsters.

"My objective is to be the head of a publishing enterprise that is in need of strong, knowledgeable leadership.

"In order to further uncover my qualifications to your satisfaction I welcome any questions you might like to ask."

Such a broadside has disarmed your interrogator. He is apt to say, "Slow down. Let's take this in smaller doses," and you have your opportunity to give chapter and verse for each of your separate accomplishments.

30 "What was the last book you read? Last play you saw?" Such questions are intended to gauge the breadth and nature of your outside interests. Are you a part of the contemporary scene or are you withdrawn into past events and experiences? Advice: expatiate on any outside interests you have, whether in direct answer to the question or not. The question merely attempts to draw you out with respect to your nonvocational activities as a measurement of your total personality. If all of your interests are work-oriented, you may have a narrow outlook, perhaps be dull, and possibly be a poor manager.

31 "What is your philosophy of management?" Millions of words and thousands of books have been written on this subject. A brief answer might be: efficiency, invention, innovation, alertness to all relevant trends, enlightenment, fairness to stockholders and employees, firmness to withstand what is disadvantageous, management by exception, management by holistic analysis to the degree possible, management to make a profit, management by ethical standards, management by objective. The more you read about and participate in the practice of management, the more eloquently and easily you can speak on this subject.

32 "Have you ever fired anyone? Why?" As a manager, you have probably had this experience. You may have had to fire someone for a reason with which you did not agree. Regardless of the reason, the question is intended to give the interviewer additional information about you and how you operate. Give an example that reflects favorably on you.

Example: Employee X had been with the company for 20 years. He was an excellent manager in an area where customers could be very appreciative of his subordinates' activities in their behalf, which were at the same time beneficial to the company. Some years ago he accepted a small gift from a customer. Subsequently, as a matter of policy the company notified all customers that gifts could not be accepted by company employees. It was recently discovered that some of this manager's subordinates were accepting large gifts from customers for special favors that they could extend without the manager's knowledge. You had to fire the manager for two reasons: (1) he had at one time accepted a gift that, as a manager, he should have known not to accept, and (2) as a manager, he should have been aware of his subordinates' activities.

33 "Have you hired people? What do you look for?" You look for individuals who will meet the standards of the position. The standards can vary. Not every individual is qualified for management; not every job leads to the top. Sometimes a position calls for a person who is not highly motivated—a plugger rather than a race horse. Continuous promotion for every employee is impossible. Some Indians do not become chiefs; some bellhops remain bellhops instead of becoming hotel managers. In answering this question you express your cognizance of the realities of corporate life.

34 "What size budget are you accustomed to administering?" A manager knows his departmental budget. Inasmuch as a budget is usually dealt with only a few times a year, refresh your memory about budget details before an interview. You should know the percentage of your budget to sales or revenue. You should know the major elements in your budget. In marketing, for example: selling, advertising, support material, administration, warehousing, and other major elements.

More Interview Questions, Pertinent and Impertinent

What do you look for in a job, security or challenge?

"I look for challenge and hope that the successful meeting of that challenge will lead to some security. I don't feel that anyone can work at his best level if he is constantly worried about whether his boss likes him, or if the company is going to prosper, or if the company is going to be sold, or if the job is going to be discontinued. A company has certain obligations to provide challenges or to let an employee know that he is not performing at a satisfactory level."

Why were your grades so low?

"When I went to college I had no objective in mind. My average was low, but I did get good grades in the subjects I was interested in."

"I participated in a great many extracurricular activities. (Explain.)

"I had to earn the money for my education, and unfortunately the work I found to do was very time consuming."

"I am attending graduate school and my grades are now superior."

"I was a poor student until I suddenly became motivated by my professor in (history) (economics) (literature) (philosophy) (other), but it was then too late to raise my average."

"In college I was not a good student. Since I have been working I have achieved an outstanding record." (Cite achievements.)

Why haven't you been more successful?

This is a tough question. Perhaps you *have* been successful, but your questioner doesn't recognize it. If so, set him straight.

Perhaps your background shows that you have changed jobs too often. Maybe you did so because you have been unlucky in your choices of employment. This is why you are so interested in the company you are visiting. Your research has shown what a fine company it is. Or possibly you were late in maturing. Many people are. You have now grown up. Or you discovered your disadvantages and returned to school to rectify them. Or you had a bad domestic environment, which is now corrected. Or as a single person you had too much fun. You are now married and settled down. Or you have recently recognized former deficiencies and have corrected them.

Explain the past in the most logical way you can and be affirmative about the future.

Why didn't you finish school?

You couldn't afford to, but you plan to do so now. You left school to enter military service. You didn't realize your career would develop as it has, and although you did not officially finish school you have studied the requirements of your position and handle them in a superior way; in fact, you supervise a number of (B.A.'s) (M.B.A.'s) (Ph.D.'s) (other).

You have learned more on the job than you could have in school. Cite your accomplishments.

Tell me about your most important achievements?

You should be able to recite them unhesitantly from having developed a résumé in which your achievements should be the most prominent part.

INTERVIEW EXAMPLES

Tell me about some of your accomplishments.

"I increased the sales of our company by eight times in a period of nine years." This may have appeared in your résumé in this manner, and for their purpose is a good statement.

But it is an unsatisfactory answer at an interview. The interviewer wants to know how you did it, hear how you express yourself, find out what kind of manager you are, and also wants to get some ammunition himself, if possible, for questions that may trip you up.

Here is the way you should answer the question at an interview:

"During my tenure at Swan and Cook Manufacturing Company as vice-president and general marketing manager, I had been able to double our sales in about five years. It still seemed to me, however, that there was a further potential of some magnitude. I spent a considerable amount of time studying our statistics—measuring distribution against population and demographics, analyzing variations on product sales by customer and a lot of other comparisons. When I started I really didn't know exactly what I was looking for.

"A pattern finally began to emerge. We had about 30 categories of products. Of these, five were in strong demand, and each had characteristics and uses that were different from the others.

"It seemed to me that we could build a consumer campaign around these five products. I assigned jobs to our inside sales department: devise a display, create an advertisement, dummy up some catalog pages, develop a formal sales presentation. When this was put together we spent a couple of days practicing among ourselves in making a sound sales presentation suitable for various kinds of buyers—wholesale and retail.

"When the plan was ready, I asked for a special meeting of the executive committee and presented the whole program, from concept to plan of execution.

"The committee was enthusiastic. We brought our salesmen in and presented the idea, and set up a plan to have home-office sales executives travel for three or four days with each salesman.

"The idea worked so well that after a few days our salesmen were able to sell the plan to nine out of ten of their customers.

"It became necessary, because of the overwhelming response, to withdraw customer presentations from most territories and confine ourselves to a few regions, until we could meet production projections.

"The end result was a tripling of our business over a period of three years. Our greatest handicap was making enough of the selected products."

Tell me about some of your accomplishments.

"Our U.K. division, where I was placed in charge, had lost $250,000 in the first quarter of 1979. I analyzed the situation and by August I had been able to reverse this trend and create earnings of $80,000."

This is obviously a valuable achievement, but is not the kind of an answer an interviewer is looking for. Here is the expanded answer that the interviewer wants to hear. It shows how you took hold decisively, made judgments, called on past experience, provided leadership:

"As vice-president and general manager of my company, a $45 million tobacco machinery manufacturer, I had responsibility for the operation of several overseas divisions.

"The U.K. division had lost $250,000 in the first quarter of 1979. By August I had turned that division around with earnings to that point of $80,000.

"My analysis had pointed up several adverse factors. For example, our payroll was overstaffed with U.S. personnel. I was able to reduce this by $235,000 without affecting the operation.

"I found that several new products had been considered, but nothing more had been done. I interjected myself into the planning and soon discovered that some of our U.S. headquarters technology could be adapted. Briefly, we did this and introduced three new products that were profitable.

"We were now in a position to expand our distribution rather than restrict it. At the same time I drew up a five-year plan and started implementing it. This started an immediate response among employees, which further added to our forward momentum, and today that U.K. division is one of our most profitable.

"As a function of this program our return on investment reached 19%."

You can be a smart and successful manager, but if you can't express why you are, you will not have successful interviews.

What you write about yourself in a good résumé or letter is the basis of what you say in an interview, expanded by the details of your accomplishments—how you recognized what needed to be done and what you did.

A résumé is a brief recapitulation. An interview is the opportunity to expand upon it. If you can express yourself as these two people did, you are ready for any interview.

Why can't we get any favorable references?

You will have a good idea why this is so, if it is. There can be both good and bad reasons. If the reasons are unfavorable to you, you have a handicap. Should you be unable to get good references from anyone, throw yourself on the mercies of your questioner, explain in detail, and give evidence that, with respect to whatever occurred, you have learned your lesson and reformed. Provide references, if possible, from church, doctor, and friends (nonbusiness references) to overcome the bad impression of your business references. If the reasons are vindictive on the part of a former employer, explain them. You may also have a basis for legal action.

If an interviewer asks you to describe your job growth, refer to your résumé, which you should know by heart.

Why didn't you go to graduate school?

I needed to earn money to get married (to repay my family for my college education) (to repay my government loan). I think I will learn more on the job. I am taking graduate studies at night. From what I read, students in graduate school gain much more from this education after a few years of experience in business. I plan to pursue and complete graduate studies in evening classes.

All these answers are adequate, responsive, and persuasive.

HINTS ON PREPAREDNESS

Be ready to express yourself in answer to the question, "Tell me about yourself." Write your answer ahead of time.

Know the names and authors of some books or articles you have read recently.

Know what salary (compensation) level you expect. At lower organizational levels salaries can range 20% plus or minus a median. At the highest organizational levels, compensation can have spreads of several hundred thousand dollars. If appropriate, study help wanted advertising to be aware of salary ranges in your specialty.

Know exactly what to say when asked why you left or are leaving your most recent or present employment.

Be sure you can detail your most important accomplishments or skills, with examples of how you achieved them or how you used them.

Develop an attitude of assurance. Conduct practice interviews.

Don't make interview dates late in the afternoon if you have a choice. Your interviewer might become restive worrying about being late for dinner.

If you are a social drinker, avoid partying the night before.

Make a list of references and have them readily available if asked for them.

Carry your résumé with you so you can leave a copy with your interviewer if asked; take such other props as may be relevant or necessary.

Review all the questions in this section and know in advance what your answers would be.

If your interview takes place on a rainy day and you have a choice between walking or riding take the transportation that will deliver you dry and closest to your destination.

Try to read an annual report on the company to which you are invited for an interview before you meet your interviewer.

If *Who's Who* or some other source can supply you with personal information about your interviewer, look it up. There may be some advantage in it.

Make sure you know all the responsibilities that normally attach to the position you are seeking. Companies assign responsibilities in different ways. Your experience may have omitted duties that would normally be expected to be part of a particular job classification. Departmental responsibility varies from campany to company particularly relative to distribution, research and development, purchasing, advertising, national and regional sales, overseas marketing, importation, acquisition and merger, and government relations, for example.

If your interview is a luncheon or dinner meeting, try to assure enough time for discussion after eating. It is hard to be suitably expressive while chewing and most people prefer to get down to brass tacks after the meal has been completed—perhaps at the coffee stage or in the beginning at the cocktail period. Ask your partner what he or she plans to select. If no first course is ordered, follow suit, and similarly with dessert. You can avoid a course, but you should not have one that your companion does not order.

Be pressed, shaved or trimmed, combed, freshly shirted, with shined shoes; or coiffed, manicured, lightly perfumed, lipsticked, powdered, accessoried, and neat.

QUESTIONS YOU CAN ASK

There are a number of questions that you can ask at a job interview:

- May I see a copy of the job description?
- Whom would I be working for and with?
- Where would I appear on the organization chart? (If position is appropriate to this question.)
- What is the growth rate of the company?
- May I have a copy of the annual report?
- If I am productive, what would I have to look forward to in further career development
- What are your major markets?
- Who are your biggest competitors?
- Who is your biggest customer in this area?
- What qualities do you want most in the position for which you are considering me?
- How soon will you make up your mind about me?
- Would you like to have a list of references? (If the question is not asked of you.)
- What are the employee benefits?
- How much travel would you consider normal for this position?
- Might relocation be required at this time or in the future?

AFTER THE INTERVIEW

Follow an interview with a letter addressed to the individual with whom you talked. Thank him or her for courtesies extended; express your continuing interest, ask for a decision. If there is no response within a few days, telephone your interviewer to find out what is happening; offer to supply additional information or to appear for another personal meeting.

INTERVIEW FAILURES

A young man, Jack Williams, went to an interview for a job as sales and advertising manager of a large company in the industry of which he was a part. He worked for a much smaller company and had an excellent record. His employer, a closely held family company, did not disclose figures, even budgets, to any except officers of the company, of whom Jack was not one, despite having an influence on company sales and profits exceeding that of any of the owners. During the interview Jack was asked the amount of his advertising budget. He floundered. He didn't know because when he wanted an appropriation he asked for and usually received it, project by project. He should have estimated the budget. He did some quick mental arithmetic and finally came up with a figure, but his obvious discomfort with the question signaled more questions on the breakdown of the budget, which he could not answer. The candidate was unsuccessful in this job application, as you can guess.

A recent graduate, an accounting major, approached the senior partner of a public accounting firm for a job. He was personable and seemed qualified until his interviewer asked the simple question, "What is your definition of the general ledger?" The candidate could not answer the question. This seems incredible, but was reported to me by the man involved in the interview.

The head of a prestigious executive recruiting firm in New York took Rod Wilson, an up-and-coming young executive, to lunch at his university club. After lunch he told Rod he was going to introduce him to some executives of a company looking for someone just like Rod to run the marketing division. The meeting was arranged after very little further conversation, and Rod met two company executives. They seemed up in the air about the nature of their quest, putting more emphasis on their acquisition interests than anything else, and the whole interview was a mess from beginning to end. The planning was poor on all sides.

A young man wrote in his résumé that he had successfully conducted a vertically integrated business, a term he had learned during his M.B.A. studies. Upon questioning, it developed that what he meant was that while attending graduate school, he sold junk merchandise part time to retailers and wholesalers in a Lower East Side New York flea market. There was nothing wrong with his work, but the description he used was misleading and therefore a mistake.

A candidate for a top-level management position, Jim Laird, was invited, with his wife, to have dinner with his prospective employer and his wife. There was a round of cocktails. Everyone seemed to be enjoying the occasion. The first round extended to three.

Jim was encouraged to talk about himself. He became expansive and boastful. He told how he grew up in a poor family, how he worked hard to raise his status until he finally achieved his present good position; how he fired his entire staff upon taking the job; how his bosses had never fully appreciated him or let him have his own way, which he was sure would be extremely good for his company. He explained that in his present job he was forced to make certain decisions within company policy when he really wanted to change the policy. (The company he was working for was very successful, the original reason for his being considered for this new position.)

He extended the conversation to tell about his education, how he met his wife, what his ambitions were, and that the people he worked for never really understood him. He explained that his authority had recently been curtailed, which was the reason he was willing to make a change in employment. When the time came to order dinner, Jim consulted with his host who recommended beef tartare. Jim, thinking to compliment his host's discriminating palate, ordered the same entrée, but added to the waiter "well done"! In the meantime, the candidate's wife recounted to her hostess how much trouble she had keeping domestic help, and that their college-age son had a drug problem.

The man was not quite as bad as he made himself appear, but he had lost his self-control. He had permitted his host to lead him into disclosures that revealed a hidden and unattractive personality and other inadequacies. His wife, nervous about what her husband was saying, chattered on. The family standards came into question. A psychologist would say that Jim had an overdeveloped fear of failure.

Epilogue: The candidate did not get the job.

In truth, it seems that there is no way to pinpoint why some interviews result in employment and some do not. We know more about what a candidate should not do than we know about what, among apparently equally qualified people, a candidate should do. We have also seen that the ratio of interviews to "hires" is about 5 to 1.

Being hired is much like getting married. Among our friends and acquaintances one often says "What did he see in her?" or vice versa. "Why did she ever marry that bum?" or vice versa. Just as in the ordinary course of events there is a man for every woman and a woman for every man, so it is in hiring. Interviewers will sometimes choose the seemingly most unlikely candidates.

We do know that these traits are affirmative:

Assurance—just the right amount.

Fluency in expressing oneself, but not glibness.

A record of accomplishment, but maybe a few minor weaknesses.

Education—but not too much, like Ph.D.'s out of context.

Personality—but what is personality?

Good appearance—but not too good.

Enthusiasm without eagerness.

We know that these traits are negative:

Sloppy appearance.

Over aggressiveness.

Lack of qualification.

Inadequate education.

Advanced age.

Unresponsiveness.

Inarticulateness.

All these factors, pro and con, are generalities and fail to reach the central reasons for an interview's success or failure. The central reason for either success or failure lies in the intangible interaction of two people. Prepare yourself for as many interview eventualities as possible. Expect that, even so, only one interview in five will be successful. Therefore get as many interviews as possible. The fact that four people out of five don't want to "marry" you is perfectly normal. The fifth individual may want to "marry" you so much it hurts; and it's the fifth one who is important unless *you* are in love with one of the other four, which is an age-old reason for social unhappiness. The difference between work and marriage is that you must work and marriage is optional.

REFLECTIONS AND REVIEW

Personal experience leads to these reflections about employment, getting it, and keeping it:

- In general, all managerial grades are screened first by résumés because they save interview time; any manager who will expose himself to a two- or three-hour interview without prior knowledge of the candidate is crazy.
- Managers at the highest levels (and some others) are most frequently hired:

1   As a result of display help wanted advertising inviting a résumé response (attempts to avoid this system by candidate telephone calls or by other methods are resisted, but some sift through).

2   By referrals from friends, acquaintances, or employees, or people with influence (knowing someone).

3   Through the offices of an executive search firm, or as a result of a company's accounting or consulting firm recommendation.

4   From unsolicited résumés, letters, or proposals.

- Department managers frequently know what they want better than the personnel department, but the latter will be responsible for finding and screening the several suitable candidates who may then be referred to the department manager for the actual hiring decision.

- In a labor-intensive company the personnel department can be so busy with labor grades, or so oriented to that kind of employment, that it has no responsibility for other than blue-collar and clerical hiring.

- In giant companies the top officers will seldom participate in employment decisions except at the highest levels, and then only after all the necessary screening has been completed by others.

- In big companies personnel executives have been upgraded to top organizational status and are of increasing influence in all hiring decisions.

- Many large, mature companies have fewer openings at mid-level and in upper management than might be expected, because of a policy to promote from within.

- Jobs at mid-level and in upper management are frequently easier to get with smaller companies (up to $15 million), at salaries comparable to those paid by big companies.

- Well-written letters will sometimes replace résumés; at all upper levels, if you want to gain the attention of a top manager by writing, you must use a letter approach; résumés are automatically routed to the personnel department, as they should be.

- In very large companies, special personnel offices are set up for the sole purpose of screening higher-level job candidates.

- At various time periods and in some geographical areas, certain types of executives are in strong demand, while in other times and places they are in oversupply; for example, for engineers, accountants, economists, financial officers, marketing officers, and generalists the demand fluctuates from year to year and is pendulum-like in operation.

- The increase in the number of M.B.A. graduates and their employment, the increase in women managers, the trend toward promoting from within, and the growing number of acquisitions have had an unfavorable impact on the hiring of mature executives, particularly in strongly established companies.

- *After age 45 one should never leave existing employment before getting another job* (unless financially secure or widely known). Age 45 is rather arbitrary; it could just as well be 48 or 55 or 43.

- If you are conducting a mail campaign for a job (and if you are employed, this is the most effective way), never address the heads of giant companies; they are not interested in you at your approach stage.

- If you are conducting a mail campaign, make it comprehensive— 500 to 1000 companies; don't use half measures. However, careful selection can improve the response and reduce the size of the mailing.

- Any job search is affected by the time you can devote to it, your age, your accomplishments, your particular field, the time of year, the state of the economy, and many other factors; it must be adjusted accordingly.

- The M.B.A. degree is a great advantage to the job seeker.

- The liberal arts degree, downgraded in recent years, is nevertheless a splendid base upon which to superimpose specialized education.

- If writing is an important method of soliciting a job, the quality of the writing is of vital importance.

- Much hiring for entry and lower-level administrative, retail sales, and similar positions is done on the basis of walk-in visits to personnel departments.

- In smaller companies (up to $10–$15 million), the head of the company may become personally involved in hiring decisions, except at the lowest levels.

- Many obscure companies employ 1000 to 5000 people and are good targets for employment applications because they are not bombarded with résumés.

- Rapidly growing companies should be primary targets of job seekers; they have had no time to establish management depth.

- Many fine companies are omitted from well-known industrial directories because they have been absorbed in acquisitions; local telephone directories will often turn up large companies that are missing from *Dun & Bradstreet* and *Standard & Poor's*.

- Large diversified companies remain a good target for employment because they are frequently composed of small divisions; if what you offer seems interesting, your résumé or correspondence may be circulated among many other divisions; the personnel department is invaluable in this respect; too much has been written about avoiding personnel departments.

- Do not be upset if you are interrogated by a person at a lower level than your own; this is an essential time-saver in a large corporation.

- For corporations that list (in directories) an assistant to a president (or chairman or other top executive), address yourself to him/her rather than to the top executive; screening you is part of his/her job.

- Going over the head of an existing manager by writing to or talking with the chairman or president can be irksome, irritating, or insulting to a departmental manager and can be the "kiss of death" to your job hopes; on the other hand, if you have something truly unusual to offer, go to the top.

- Overaggressiveness displayed in conversation or letters will be included in any assessment of you and would be a detriment to your employment in many companies; some people like aggressiveness, others hate it; you can be aggressive in technique, but not in style.

- Financial people such as accountants, treasurers, controllers, and corporation counsels can apply to almost any company for employment, regardless of what it makes or does; marketing and production people more often need to choose companies related to their experience.

- Very small industries should be avoided even if a job often sounds good; there is no place to go if the industry doesn't grow or if technological change overcomes it.

- For maximum career progress and job-getting ability avoid career gaps: a year off to travel or write a book, activity as a self-employed consultant over a period of a couple of years, or any self-employment that you do not expect to continue.

- Make a habit of thinking about yourself on a regular basis, review your accomplishments, keep a continuing record of them in writing.

- Plan steps to remove yourself from any company in which you are stymied through no fault of your own; on the other hand, offers implicit in "afraid to quit?" advertising by career advisers are dangerous invitations.

- Competition for jobs is keen; make sure you really have something to offer before you offer yourself as a job candidate.

- Most jobs are never advertised; you can only find out about them by advertising your availability (résumés, letters, other writings, investigations, visits, referrals by others).

- The lower the level at which you apply for a job, the easier it is to get one, and vice versa.

- Many people find jobs by a lucky chance or by being in the right place at the right time; you can give luck a chance to be on your side by circulating the fact of your availability.

- Never become so involved in your job that you don't have time to think about yourself.

- Never hesitate to seek advice, if needed; even if it is expensive it may be very cheap in terms of your career development.

- Even if you are secure in your job, plan for what you would do if you lost it; there is more uncertainty in any job now than at any time in the past.

- The expansion of government carries with it the enlargement of job opportunities in government; many companies welcome former government employees who can help find paths through government bureaucracies.

- It frequently requires as much as a year of hard work to find a new job.

- An expression of your availability and your skills might open up a job for which no search is actually in progress or contemplated; there is no way to know without trying.

- Marketable skills are to be found in your accomplishments; you have to be sure that you have and suitably identify tangible and important accomplishments before offering them for sale.

- Employment letters to top executives of large companies marked "confidential" or "personal" are sometimes irritants to the addressee, particularly to the heads of major corporations. In general they should be avoided.

- In 1978, 3.5 million new jobs opened up.

- If unemployment is 6%, there remains a 94% chance of finding the job you want (if you are qualified).

- Companies in need of management talent are just as interested in hiring as you are in getting a job; therefore if you express yourself in such a way as to expose your possession of a needed talent, your job search will be greatly facilitated.

- Executives or those hoping to be executives should not permit their activities in a present job to become so narrow in scope that they become specialists in an area of little use to other companies. Examples: attorneys dealing with nuclear regulatory agencies; systems analysts for very small companies; utility rate experts; supervisors of small departments (order handling, customer service); certain specialized banking jobs.

- From time to time return to academia to brush up on new management techniques; knowledge accumulates in geometrical progression every five or ten years.

- If you are in a 60–70% tax bracket, consider hiring a *personal* assistant out of your own pocket to provide expertise in areas in which you may be weak.

- Analyze your talents and your work preferences in anticipation of the possibility of a second career.

- Always learn how to handle the next job above you and the one above that as well.

- As you grow older make an increasing effort to review regularly what you are doing and what you have done in order to discover how it can be done better; executives are replaced or downgraded because they have become complacent.

- Preparation time in advance of an interview should be about two hours for every half-hour of interview time expected.

- Cease all interview preparation 24 hours before the interview and think about something else.

- Employers tend to overestimate the qualifications necessary for adequate job performance; and candidates usually offer less than is wanted.

- Job candidates miss out on job opportunities more often for lack of interview preparation than for lack of qualifications.

- Interviewer misjudgment is the cause of both excessive job turnover and weak employee selection.

- More people fail in their jobs as a result of their own or their boss's personality defects than for lack of competence.

- There are billions of dollars of profit-making productivity going to waste as a result of corporate disinclination to employ mature executives.

- If the awarding of jobs were based on an accurate assessment of qualifications existing at the time of appointment, there would never be, for example, a President of the United States; people create their qualifications on the job if they are any good—or crack up in the process.
- There are no absolutes in any of the foregoing statements.

AFTER YOU GET THE JOB

The following is excerpted from *Korn/Ferry International's Executive Profile: A Survey of Corporate Leaders*, based on a survey of 1708 senior functional and specialist managers in Fortune 500 companies.

A TYPICAL EXECUTIVE

He was born in 1926 and spent most of his childhood in the urban Midwest. Eldest of three children, he attended public schools, helped put himself through college (a large public institution) by working part time, and then earned his M.B.A. at a top private university. He started with his employer 19 years ago as a functional specialist. He is married, has three children, and his wife has no outside career; his family has had to relocate during his career, but not often.

He believes concern for results, integrity, and desire for responsibility increase one's chances for success—more so than creativity, ambition, and aggressiveness. And he should know. Though he may never assume the company presidency—and he doesn't seek it—his success is indisputable, because these preponderant characteristics describe a senior executive of America's largest corporations.

How These Executives Started Their Careers

Marketing/sales	27%
Finance/accounting	60%
Professional/technical	30%

Percentage of these executives in general management now:

Of those starting in Marketing/sales	52%
Of those starting in Finance/accounting	31%
Of those starting in Professional/technical	51%

Fastest routes to the top as reported by these executives:

Finance/accounting	33%
Marketing/sales	31%
Professional/technical	7%

Reasons for Success

Biggest single factor was noted as follows:

Hard work	17.5%
Ambition, drive	9.4%
Getting along with others	9.6%

Traits that Enhance Executive Success

Concern for results	73.7%
Integrity	66.3
Desire for responsibility	57.8
Concern for people	49.2
Creativity	44.7

Average yearly compensation of Respondents: $116,000
Political persuasion of respondents:

Republican	68%
Democrat	13%
Independent	18%

Average years employed by same company: 19
Number of companies worked for, average: 3
Reasons for changing jobs:

Increased responsibility	44.0%
Increased challenge	42.0%
Better compensation	31.9%

The complete survey is available from Korn/Ferry International, 277 Park Ave., New York, NY 10017, for $7.50.

INDEX